ANAXIMANDER, HERACLIT[...]
PLOTINUS, LAO-TZU, NAGARJUNA

Other books by Karl Jaspers in English translation

THE FUTURE OF MANKIND

THE IDEA OF THE UNIVERSITY

TRUTH AND SYMBOL

MAN IN THE MODERN AGE

REASON AND EXISTENZ

THE ORIGIN AND GOAL OF HISTORY

TRAGEDY IS NOT ENOUGH

REASON AND ANTI-REASON IN OUR TIME

THE WAY TO WISDOM

THE PERENNIAL SCOPE OF PHILOSOPHY

THE QUESTION OF GERMAN GUILT

THE GREAT PHILOSOPHERS: THE FOUNDATIONS

GENERAL PSYCHOPATHOLOGY

NIETZSCHE AND CHRISTIANITY

PHILOSOPHY AND THE WORLD

THREE ESSAYS: LEONARDO, DESCARTES, MAX WEBER

THE NATURE OF PSYCHOTHERAPY

NIETZSCHE: AN INTRODUCTION TO THE UNDERSTANDING
OF HIS PHILOSOPHICAL ACTIVITY

THE FUTURE OF GERMANY

PHILOSOPHY IS FOR EVERYMAN

NIETZSCHE: AN INTRODUCTION TO HIS
PHILOSOPHICAL ACTIVITY

THE PHILOSOPHY OF EXISTENCE

KARL JASPERS

ANAXIMANDER
HERACLITUS
PARMENIDES
PLOTINUS
LAO-TZU
NAGARJUNA

From *The Great Philosophers: The Original Thinkers*

Edited by Hannah Arendt

Translated by Ralph Manheim

A Harvest Book

HBJ

A HELEN AND KURT WOLFF BOOK

HARCOURT BRACE JOVANOVICH

New York and London

Printed in the United States of America

Library of Congress Cataloging in Publication Data

Jaspers, Karl, 1883-1969.
Anaximander, Heraclitus, Parmenides, Plotinus, Lao-tzu, Nagarjuna.

(A Harvest book, HB 288)
"A Helen and Kurt Wolff book."
Previously published as part of v. 2 of the author's
The great philosophers, which is a translation of
Die grossen Philosophen.
Bibliography: p.
1. Philosophers, Ancient. I. Title.
[B113.J3713]   180   74-4335

ISBN 0-15-607500-8

First Harvest edition 1974
A B C D E F G H I J

Acknowledgments

Acknowledgment is made for permission to use the following: For the quotations from *Early Greek Philosophy* by J. Burnet, Barnes & Noble, Inc., and A. & C. Black Ltd. For the quotations from *The Way of Lao Tzu*, translated by Wing-tsit Chan, copyright © 1963, The Bobbs-Merrill Company, Inc. For the quotations from Plotinus: *The Enneads* (third edition), translated by Stephen MacKenna, Faber and Faber Ltd. and Pantheon Books, a Division of Random House, Inc. For the quotations from *Plato and Parmenides,* translated with Introduction and running commentary by Francis Macdonald Cornford, Humanities Press and Routledge & Kegan Paul Ltd.

CONTENTS

ANAXIMANDER   3

HERACLITUS AND PARMENIDES   9

HERACLITUS

1. The *logos*   11
2. Struggle, the salutary way   14
3. Characterization   17
4. Influence   17

PARMENIDES

1. Being   19
2. The world of appearance   22
3. The decision   23
4. The insoluble difficulties   24
5. Influence   25

COMPARISON BETWEEN HERACLITUS AND PARMENIDES

1. Their common situation   28
2. The common new element in their thinking   28
3. Agreement and opposition   29
4. Pure thought   29
5. Prophecy and will to power   30
6. Historical appraisal   31

PLOTINUS

I. Life and works   32

II. Description of the Plotinian "System"   34
   A. Matter and the One   34
   B. The scale of beings   35

      c. The categories   *35*

      D. Spirit, soul, nature   *36*

      E. Descent and ascent   *37*

III. Transcending as a Whole   *41*

IV. The Stages of Knowledge   *45*

 V. Speculative Transcending   *50*

      1. The categories   *51*

      2. Categorial transcending   *52*

      3. Transcending in images of the All   *63*

VI. Fall and Resurgence   *63*

      A. Necessity and freedom   *65*

      B. Twofold guilt and twofold freedom   *66*

      c. Evil   *67*

      D. The two souls   *68*

      E. The twofold longing   *69*

      F. The situation of the soul in the world   *70*

      G. Philosophy is ascent to the One   *71*

VII. Against Materialism and Gnosis   *73*

VIII. Critical Characterization   *77*

      A. Contradictions   *77*

      B. Empirical knowledge and mythical conceptions   *78*

      c. The existential meaning   *79*

IX. Historical Position and Influence   *83*

LAO-TZU

Life and Works   *87*

  I. Exposition of Lao-tzu's Philosophy   *88*

      1. The Tao   *88*

      2. Tao and world   *90*

      Cosmogony and the process of the individual in the world   *92*

      3. Tao and the individual (ethics)   *93*

      4. Tao and government   *101*

II. Characterization and Criticism   *107*

    1. The meaning of Lao-tzu   *107*

    2. Lao-tzu's successors   *110*

    3. Lao-tzu's historical position and limitations   *113*

NAGARJUNA

    I. The Operations of Thought   *115*

    Summary of the Doctrine   *119*

    II. The Meaning of the Doctrine   *120*

    Historical Comparisons   *130*

    Bibliography   *133*

    Index of Names   *137*

ANAXIMANDER, HERACLITUS, PARMENIDES,
PLOTINUS, LAO-TZU, NAGARJUNA

ANAXIMANDER

Anaximander (c. 610–546) was a citizen of Miletus, the largest of the Ionian commercial centers and as such a gathering point of knowledge emanating from the Mediterranean regions and the Near East. Empirical knowledge and technical skills were reflected in navigation, commerce, colonial undertakings, temple architecture, and such enterprises as the tunnel built by Eupalinos on Samos. Anaximander was said to have directed the founding of a colony on the Black Sea (Apollonia). He was said to have demonstrated, in Sparta, a *gnomon,* or sun dial, imported from Babylonia. He was sixty-four, and his work was complete, when the Persian invasion put an end to Ionian freedom.

Anaximander was the first man to draw a map of the earth (*geographia*) and to construct a celestial globe (*sphaira*); the first to conceive the clear and simple idea, so revolutionary for his time because it contradicted immediate perception, that the earth floated free in cosmic space and that the sun and stars were moving on the other side of it between their setting and rising; thanks to his radical, constructive imagination, he was the first to represent the cosmos, both in its form and in its movements, as a coherent whole. And he was also the first thinker to develop, in concepts, a metaphysical vision transcending all sense perception; the first to give the name of the Divine to what is achieved in the fundamental thinking that transcends all that exists, or, in other words, to find the divine with the help of thought, instead of accepting it as given in traditional religious conceptions. He was the first Greek to find in prose the appropriate form in which to communicate such insights. And he effected all these momentous innovations of human consciousness quietly, without polemics against anyone.

His starting point was an empirical knowledge which, by primitive standards, was already considerable. It provided him with material for projections that reached out ahead of what he knew. Based on the notion of proportional reduction, his map of the earth was a speculative geometrical construction filled in with the meager and diffuse data supplied by Ionian navigators. Thus it was soon superseded as more reliable data became available. The greatness lay in the general conception and in the discovery of a principle of representation. Anaximander mapped not only the inhabited earth but also the cosmos as a whole—he did so without empirical proofs, on the basis of his inner vision, proceeding in accordance with the un-formulated principle that the whole cosmos in all its parts must be subject to the same spatial and numerical relations as the things we perceive around us. In his view the earth has the shape of a cylinder, a kind of truncated column, its thickness equal to one-third the diameter of its surface. We live on the one surface. The earth is suspended in the center of the cosmos, at rest because there is nothing to cause it to move. Around it the heavens form a sphere (and no longer a bowl), or rather, three concentric spheres, the sphere of the stars, which is closest to the earth, and those of the moon and the sun, at intervals of 9, 18, and 27 diameters of the earth. There is no absolute above and below.

This world came into being. After the separation of hot and cold, a part of the cold damp interior was transformed into vapor by the heat of the fiery sphere, and the vapor split the fiery sphere into rings. These rings cloaked in vapor have breathing holes through which the flames shine. These are the stars, the moon, and the sun. On the earth everything was at first moist. The sun dried out some of the moisture. The evaporation created wind. The remaining moisture was the sea, which became smaller and smaller and will, in the end, disappear altogether. Eclipses of the heavenly bodies occur when the air holes are temporarily stopped up; the phases of the moon are caused by a slow closing and reopening of the holes (Burnet).

Living creatures sprang from the moisture. The first were encased in a prickly bark. Some moved to the dry land, the bark fell away, and they changed their form of life. Man developed from animals of another species. For if he had been originally as he is now, he would never have survived. Unlike the animals, who from birth can find their food by themselves, he alone requires a long period of suckling. Originally, says Anaximander, man was similar to a fish.

There are innumerable worlds such as ours, coexisting at equal intervals; and all these worlds, including ours, come into being and pass away in periodic recurrence. The destruction of our world will be followed by a regeneration.

Such views are imputed to Anaximander by other writers. Only one sentence, though introduced in indirect discourse, is quoted verbatim, and its content is entirely different. This venerable monument runs: Anaximander said that "the material cause and first element (*archē*) of existing things was the infinite (*apeiron*); but the source from which existing things derive their existence is also that to which they return at their destruction according to necessity; for they must pay the penalty and make atonement to one another for their injustice according to Time's decree." This sentence formulates a metaphysical vision. We do not know whether it is a maxim or, as seems likelier, a fragment of a larger exposition. In attempting to understand it we are under a disadvantage—we cannot help operating with the rigid concepts of later times and with our own thinking; nevertheless, with the help of what other ancient authors have written about Anaximander, let us attempt an interpretation.

1. What are existing things (*ta onta*)? Everything: the events and conditions in the polis, the stars, the water, the earth, men and animals, the totality of present things.

2. What is the *apeiron*? The meaning of the word is infinite, boundless, undetermined. Thus the *apeiron* is not an object of intuition. The ancients understood Anaximander's *apeiron* as the matter from which the worlds arise and to which they return—analogous to the water from which all things originated, according to the earlier Thales. But water was visibly present in the world. Anaximander took the leap to positing a source that was not only invisible but could not even be defined. Aristotle interprets: The one cannot be a part of what springs from it (as in the case of water). It cannot be a particular thing—if it were a particular thing, the whole could not spring from it. It must encompass (*periechein*) everything, it cannot be encompassed (*periechomenon*). Furthermore, it cannot be finite. For then becoming would have an end. In order that becoming should not cease, the ground of becoming must be infinite, inexhaustible. It is the origin of all and has itself no origin. Accordingly Anaximander calls the *apeiron* immortal and indestructible. Unlike all things in the world (*ta onta*) which come and go, it is everlasting.

3. How are the things (of the worlds) related to the *apeiron*? Simplicius writes: Anaximander "did not attribute the genesis of things to any change in matter but said that the opposites were differentiated in the substrate, which is an unlimited body." The differentiation of opposites is the origin of existing things. It seems futile to inquire further how oppositions arise in the imperishable *apeiron* that has been said to be free from opposition. The oppositions within existing things are as such insuperable. Even as I inquire, I am in them. I arrive at no better understanding by distinguishing an "eternal motion" that leads to oppositions from the motion in the existing, perpetually changing world. The emergence of things from the *apeiron* and their return to it might perhaps be distinguished from the emergence of things from one another. But whether we conceive of the *apeiron* according to later concepts as matter (with which, however, no form is contrasted), or as empty space (though without any energy to fill it), or, in accordance with the earlier view, as chaos—its essential characteristic is that while free from opposition, it is the source of oppositions. The world comes into being with the opposition between hot and cold. When the oppositions annul one another, the world will have ceased to be. The totality of things already in opposition (*ta onta*) is called *physis*. *Physis* is none of the antagonistic things but encompasses them all.

4. What is the injustice of things? By their very nature, the opposites war with one another. Once differentiated, they produce one another and

destroy one another: hot and cold, air and water, light and darkness. The predominance of one is injustice to the other. Hence they must make atonement to one another. But the *apeiron* does not participate in this struggle.

In this view certain authors (Nietzsche, Rohde) have seen an allusion to the guilt that comes of individualization, the fall from grace involved in entering existence: man's greatest guilt is having been born (Calderón). Such an interpretation is not in keeping with the general climate of this thinking, but perhaps there is a trace of truth in it. Anaximander does not impute guilt to the genesis of the world (and the birth of man is not even mentioned in this connection); but once the world has come into being, guilt is no doubt an inevitable consequence of its antagonisms.

5. How is the *apeiron* related to the world? It plays a part in the world process, for it "steers all things." But in Anaximander's simile, it is Dikē (Justice), the foundation of the polis, which imposes a balance among conflicting things by making them atone for their wrongs to one another. In the polis justice is administered and the penalty appointed by the judge. Taking this reality as his guide, Solon taught the existence of a more encompassing *dikē*, which is no longer dependent on human jurisdiction, for it will inevitably be fulfilled in the course of time. The power of Dikē is inexorable. Anaximander finds such an equilibration in the world process as a whole: things are in conflict with each other, as men in a court of justice. The penalty is meted out "according to Time's decree." But time is not itself the judge; it brings about the judgment. Time is not the *apeiron,* but the *apeiron* governs temporal events. Anaximander was the first Western thinker to conceive of the world as a community of justice, as an order among things (Jäger).

6. What is necessity? Certain writers have found in Anaximander a conception which was not to be clearly formulated until later: as cosmic law, law of nature, the necessity of process. In Anaximander things come into being and pass away "according to necessity" (the Greek words have also been translated as "according to duty" and "as it is decreed"). But this necessity is not a clearly defined natural law, open to investigation; it would be more accurate to say that by his intellectual leap Anaximander arrived at an abstraction which was later to generate the determinate idea of natural law. In Anaximander's necessity norm and causality, determination and fate, the justice of atonement and the automatism of the world process are not differentiated; nevertheless, it is superior to all the mythical explanations of events, based on the personal caprice of superhuman powers or the concept of mere chance. And Anaximander's "necessity" preserves what is lost in later thinkers who effect these differentiations, namely the metaphysical visions of what from Spinoza's "necessity" to Nietzsche's "shield of necessity" was thought to transcend all categories, or, considered as fate, became a problem inaccessible to rational thought.

7. What, in this total view of the *apeiron,* are the gods? Anaximander called the *apeiron* itself divine. Moreover, Cicero tells us: "The view of Anaximander is that the gods are not everlasting but are born and perish at long intervals of time, and that they are worlds, countless in number." We do not know whether Anaximander rebelled against the traditional faith, as later Xenophanes, Heraclitus, and Plato rejected the Homeric pantheon. With the sober detachment that enabled him to overturn all existing views, he saw the divine in a new way, but in two forms: on the one hand the *apeiron,* on the other, the plurality of worlds.

Interpretations in terms of crystallized concepts tend to see too much or too little in Anaximander—his wealth of potential meaning far exceeds all such interpretations. Beguiled by the hidden possibilities, subsequent thinkers have found all sorts of ideas in Anaximander. Some of these interpretations are demonstrably false, some can be shown to be possible, a few can be definitely substantiated.

Anaximander is the earliest philosopher perceptible as a personality, though we know him only as a shadow of himself. It was he who first entered the realm where philosophy and science in their Western forms became possible. The known contents of his thinking are no longer an indispensable element of philosophy; what speaks to us is the magnificent originality of his thinking. He is the first Western philosopher whose *style* of thought bears an unmistakable stamp.

Anaximander's profound impression on us flows from the whole of his thinking, in which we perceive the awakening of Western reason; the veils of mist are dispersed and the light is born. To his new way of thinking the simplest things were revealed that no one else had been able to think of before. Once the leap was made, man was able to reach out for the knowledge that would change his world completely. What is so exciting is the beginning as such. At this moment man first learned to look at himself and the world with detachment; thought came into its own and ventured, in defiance of custom, tradition, and appearance, to put forth ideas which at first sight may have seemed utterly absurd and sacrilegious. In rejecting all authority other than its own insights, thought penetrated to the depths.

Admirably simple, yet so radical in their implications, these steps were made possible by a threefold process of abstraction, leading first from immediate appearance, through an imaginary change of standpoint, to new representations and, through a real change of standpoint, to new perceptions (the suspension of the earth in cosmic space, the absence of an absolute above and below, the proportional reduction of the earth's surface in cartography); secondly, from all these representations to what can be definitely thought but not intuited (necessity, justice, reciprocity in opposition); and thence, finally, to what, unthinkable in determinate form, precedes the oppositions.

Wherever this thinker turns, his mind shows equal power: in his observation of the sensuous here and now, in technical invention, in his devising of convincing demonstrations, in his use of a primitive mathematics, in ordering his intuitions (even if these are unverifiable), and in the pure speculative thinking that carries him into the ground of all being. With the same energy he encompasses speculation and the world, metaphysics and empirical thinking. It is by one and the same mode of thought that he produced the map of the earth and the celestial globe, discovered that the world hung free in cosmic space, gave concrete form to his view of the genesis of the worlds, conceived of all existing things as grounded in the *apeiron,* and looked upon the *apeiron* as the divine. The mind of a great philosopher is one. No factor may be removed. In every direction of his thinking, Anaximander discloses this unity; the independence of the individual, provided by the Ionian polis, became the independence of thought which came to grips with the world and allowed things to show themselves as they are. Here we see our own Western existence as it began, manifesting itself in a grandiose prototype—a miracle, but a miracle whose content is perfectly self-evident and natural. Anaximander confronted the real world with measurement, observation, reason—in short, with the human intellect. He had the courage to formulate speculative schemas that were subject to verification; with his magnificent Ionian open-mindedness, he was alive to all the possibilities of his world.

In the ensuing period, this comprehensive thought, erupting from a world of myth, was to make possible highly varied intellectual movements: the pure speculation of Parmenides and Heraclitus, cosmic views of the world, scientific inquiry.

HERACLITUS AND PARMENIDES

Both lived at the turn of the sixth century, Heraclitus in Ephesus (Asia Minor), Parmenides in Elea (southern Italy). Since "the coming of the Medes" the Greek world of Asia Minor had lost its freedom and lived under a constant threat that was to be averted only by the Persian Wars. Anaximander's polis had undergone a change. It had ceased to enjoy undisturbed freedom in an open Mediterranean; the internal consequences of the threat were first democracy, then tyranny. Elea was a colony of Ionian Greeks who had fled from the Medes. This was the situation in which Heraclitus and Parmenides, at opposite ends of the Greek world, did their thinking; philosophically, both were rooted in the Ionian soil.

HERACLITUS

Born of an old noble family, Heraclitus ceded the inherited rights of a priest-king (*basileus*) to his younger brother. Asked by the Ephesians to give them laws, he declined, saying that bad government had already become entrenched in the city. He deposited his writings in the temple of the Ephesian Artemis.

This work, of which some one hundred and thirty fragments have come down to us, consisted of incisive, powerfully formulated maxims. They did not form a systematic edifice, but there is a unity in their mode of thought. The original arrangement cannot be reconstructed. Their succinctness invites the reader to interpret endlessly. That is why Heraclitus was known in antiquity as "the obscure."

The style is solemn, prophetic. Heraclitus speaks like a man convinced that his thinking is absolutely unprecedented and extraordinary, and that it illumines everything once and for all.

1. The logos. Heraclitus sets out to "put words and deeds to the test" by explaining "things each by its own nature and pointing out the real state of the case." Looking at the whole, he sees what is; he sees the "*logos* that is everlasting" and what it does. "All things come to pass in accordance with this *logos.*" The *logos* pervades all things and encompasses the whole of Heraclitus' thinking. *Logos* can neither be translated into any other term nor defined as a concept. *Logos* can signify: word, discourse, content of discourse, meaning; reason, truth; law; even Being. In Heraclitus it is not defined; it carries all these meanings at once and is never limited to any one of them. The *logos* is the Encompassing, undefined and endlessly definable (like all the great and basic terms of philosophy).

Always implicit in the *logos* is the unity of opposites. "Men do not understand how what is at variance agrees with itself. It is an attunement of opposite tensions like that of the bow and the lyre." "The hidden harmony is better than the visible."

The idea of the unity of opposites is stated abstractly: "Whole and not whole—drawing together and drawing apart, concord and discord . . . From all one and from one all." It is also formulated in concrete, sensuous terms: "Cold things grow hot, hot things grow cold, the wet dries, the parched is moistened." "And it is the same thing in us that is quick and dead, awake and asleep, young and old; the former by their changing become the latter, and the latter in turn are changed and become the former." Pleasure springs from its opposite: "Sickness makes health pleasant and good, hunger satisfaction, weariness rest." "It recovers through change" (or in a different translation: "In changing it takes its rest").

Opposition is life, change is necessary to life: "It is a weariness to labor for the same masters and be ruled by them." "Even the posset separates if it is not stirred." It is absurd to wish that all conflict may cease. "There would be no harmony without high and low, nor any living creatures without the opposites male and female."

Everything we know we know through its opposite. We would not know justice if there were no injustice. From different points of view, we can form diametrically opposite ideas of one and the same thing: "In the circumference of a circle beginning and end are." "For the fuller's screw, the way, straight and crooked, is one and the same." "The way up and down is one and the same." Sea water is life-giving (for fish) and destructive (for men).

In the ground of things, all is one: "Immortals are mortal, mortals are immortal; each lives the life of the other, and dies their life." Hades (death) is the same as Dionysus (jubilant life) in whose honor they rave and perform the Bacchic revels. "We are and we are not."

The *logos* is the the coming together of opposites in struggle. And yet, he who has listened to the *logos* knows that: "All things are one." In the world of opposites, that is, in the cosmos and in our existence as well: "War is king and father of all."

Heraclitus does not expressly distinguish the ways in which the opposites are linked or the ways in which one shifts into the other; he does not state clearly in what sense it is possible to speak of the identity of opposites. He is guided by his great intuition of all existence as opposition, of the unity of opposites, and finally of the godhead as the unity encompassing all opposites. He makes no attempt to formulate a logic of opposition (dialectics); his theme is his great vision: everywhere identical unity.

Thus the *logos* is the unity of opposites. It is also the source of *law* (*nomos*). Rational thought takes hold of *logos* and *nomos*. Therein lies wisdom (*to sophon*).

The *logos* is the essence of the world and the soul:

The cosmological notions developed by the Milesian thinkers provide Heraclitus with the material by which to apprehend the *logos* in the world. He was not interested in concrete investigation, but only in discerning the operation of *logos* and *nomos* in the world. For him *fire* is not merely one state of matter, side by side with water and air (in which the natural philosophers found the substance of things), but the symbol, and at the same time, the reality of world, life, and soul. Fire is the cause of cosmic order, but is itself endowed with reason (*phronimon*). "The thunderbolt (i.e. eternal fire) steers all things." The soul is fire. The more fiery it is, the more reason it has. The dry soul is wise, the moist (drunken) soul is tipsy. We breathe in the divine *logos* and become rational.

The foundation of the world is rest (eternal fire), the world itself is motion. The world is unceasing change. Everything flows and nothing remains. You cannot step twice into the same river. "It is impossible to touch the same mortal substance twice; through the rapidity of change they scatter and again combine, and separate." But the eternal flux is subject to the law of the *logos,* which is called justice (dikē). "The sun will not overstep his measures, for otherwise the Erinyes, Dikē's deputies, will find him out."

The *logos* is hidden and can become manifest: It is hidden, although it presides over all happening. "Nature (*physis*) likes to hide." All that happens is ordered according to the *logos,* even when men fail to know it and act against it. But the *logos* can be manifested to man's reason. It is not disclosed by much knowledge, but by authentic knowledge, which man can achieve only through himself. "Men have the capacity of self-knowledge and of insight." "I searched myself," said Heraclitus (in another translation: "I looked for myself"). But such insight does not yield knowledge as a possession: "You will never find the limits of the soul, though you travel in every direction, so deep is its *logos.*" Such searching brings growth, both in the knower and in the known. "The soul has its own *logos* which grows according to its needs."

The *logos* is the common bond (*to xynon*).

First: "Insight (*phronein*) is common to all." Insight is alertness. "The waking have one common world, but the sleeping turn aside each into a world of his own." Second: "War is common to all and justice is conflict; all life springs from conflict and necessity."

The common bond is elucidated in thought and action. In thinking we understand together, in acting we fulfill together. In thought the common bond of the *logos* opposes the isolating particular (*idion*). In action, the community of opposites resulting from conflict is opposed to the isolation that springs from complete rest and peace.

In Heraclitus as in most of the pre-Socratics, the gods are not the originators; they are beings in the world. "This ordered universe (cosmos), which is the same for all, was created by neither a god nor a man, it always was and is and will be ever-living fire." However, when Heraclitus speaks not of the gods, but of God (which in the language of Greek philosophy is called the God, the Divine, the gods), he speaks of him as he speaks of the Logos, the Cosmos, Fire. But there is also an intimation of a greater, more *profound vision of God:* "One thing, the Wise alone, is unwilling and yet willing to be called by the name of Zeus." The Wise steers all things, but "of all those whose teaching I have heard no one has gone far enough to teach that the Wise is something apart (*kechōrismenon*) from all things." Here the transcendent is represented as absolutely other, an idea of whose novelty and deep significance Heraclitus is fully aware.

This proudest of thinkers refers frequently to the distance between God and man. "Human nature has no insights, but the Divine has them." "Compared with man, the most beautiful ape is ugly; compared with God, the wisest of men seems like an ape in wisdom, beauty, and everything else." God's power is everywhere: "The things that crawl are protected by God's whiplash." No one can escape it. "How can anyone hide from that which never sets?"

The views of God and man are fundamentally different and incommensurable: "To God all things are beautiful, good, and just; but men have assumed some things to be unjust, others just." Men and gods are not, as in the traditional Greek religion, taken as beings of the same kind (distinguished only by mortality and immortality). Man is completely and essentially different from God.

2. *Struggle, the salutary way.* Heraclitus' vision of God and the world is no mere contemplation of eternal being; it is itself in the world, a struggle against falsehood and evil, a proclamation of the salutary way.

Accordingly Heraclitus pictures what is false in the world. Most men (*hoi polloi*) do not understand the *logos*. "They know not what they are doing when awake, just as they forget what they do in sleep." Though they are in constant association with the *logos,* they are at odds with it. What they encounter every day remains strange to them, they succumb to illusion. Nor does Heraclitus' teaching help them. "Even when they have heard, they do not understand. . . . Present, they are absent. . . ." "Even when they hear it, they fail to grasp; but they suppose they have understood."

Men are under illusion when they act, yet their actions follow the hidden *logos*. "Those who sleep are fellow workers (in the activities of the world)." Hence the twofold aspect of the human world: "Time is a child playing a game of draughts; the kingship is in the hands of a child." "Human opinions are the games of a child." But what is fortuitous and meaningless to those who do not know is actually hidden order: "A heap of rubble piled up at random is the fairest universe."

In ignorance of the *logos* but unconsciously obeying it, all things and creatures perform the appropriate actions: "Pigs wash themselves in mud, birds in dust or ashes." "Donkeys prefer chaff to gold." "A foolish man is startled at every meaningful word (*logos*)." "Dogs bark at those they do not recognize."

In practice, Heraclitus' insight into life as community in conflict is *his* struggle. He seems to attack everything in the world around him: the inherited tradition, the prevailing religion, the men and doctrines hitherto regarded as great, the political condition of his native city, the thoughtless behavior of men impelled by their passions.

1. *Against prevailing religion:* "They purify themselves by staining themselves with other blood, as if one were to step into mud to wash off mud." "They talk to statues (of the gods) as if one were to converse with buildings." He threatens the "night revelers, magicians, Bacchants, Maenads and Mystics" with punishment after death. For "the rites accepted by mankind in the Mysteries are unholy."

But often Heraclitus points to the truth in religion. "He called the shameful rites of the Mysteries remedies." He distinguished "two kinds of sacrifice; the one is offered by the few who are inwardly purified, the other is material." If the phallic cult "were not conducted in honor of Dionysos, it would be utterly shameless." And he takes a purely positive view of religion when he says: "The Sybil with raving mouth uttering her unlaughing, unadorned, unincensed words reaches out over a thousand years with her voice, for she is inspired by the God." Or: "The lord whose oracle is at Delphi, neither speaks nor conceals, but indicates."

Immortality for Heraclitus is unquestionable: "When men die, things await them that they neither expect nor imagine." "The greater the death, the greater the reward." ". . . the souls arise and become watchful guardians of the living and dead."

2. Heraclitus condemns all those *who had hitherto been regarded as great.* "Homer deserves to be thrown out of the contest and beaten; likewise Archilochos." Hesiod, Pythagoras, Xenophanes, Hecataeus all show that much knowledge does not confer reason. Pythagoras, in particular, read many books and established a wisdom of his own; he was the ancestor of all swindlers. What is the thing they called reason? "They put reliance in street singers and their teacher is the populace, for they do not know that the many are evil and that only few are good."

3. *The political condition of his city* aroused Heraclitus' anger. "The Ephesians would do well to hang themselves, every man of them, since they have expelled Hermodoros, the most valuable man among them, saying: Let us not have even one valuable man; but if we do, let him go elsewhere and live among others." "To me [on the contrary] one man is worth ten thousand if he is the best." "To obey the will of one man is also law." And he cries out bitterly: "May wealth never fail you, men of Ephesus, so that your evil may become visible." But he also states the fundamental truth of political life: "The citizens should fight for their law as if for their city wall."

4. *The struggle against the passions of the individual.* What is happiness? "If happiness lay in bodily pleasures, we should have to say that oxen were happy when they found vetch to eat." "It is not best for men to obtain everything they wish." The passions are powerful. "It is hard to fight against impulse; whatever it wishes, it buys at the expense of the soul." "Arro-

gance is more in need of quenching than fire." "He called self-conceit epilepsy."

Heraclitus combats the false and gives instruction for a life in truth. The philosopher of the *logos* bids man to be awake. "Men should not act and speak as though asleep." We should knowingly follow the hidden *logos* that binds all, not sink into the individual; nor should we let ourselves be driven unconsciously by the *logos;* we should open ourselves to the universal and partake of it knowingly; deep within the *logos* we should find the universal which is already there but becomes the common, unifying bond only in being discovered.

In regard to the true life his teaching hinges on three points: 1. Participation in the *logos* of struggle. 2. Participation in the *logos* of knowledge. 3. Fundamental knowledge.

a) "Men should know that war is common to all." "War is king and father of all. And some he has made gods and some men, some slaves and some free." The victor is free, the vanquished is a slave, and he who falls in battle is immortal. For "the best choose one thing above all else: everlasting fame rather than things mortal." Those who fall in battle are "honored by gods and men."

b) "The greatest perfection (*arētē*) resides in thinking wisely (*phronein*): to speak the truth and to act in accordance with nature (*physis*)—this is wisdom."

c) Wisdom does not reside in the heaping up of information, which makes for dispersion and distracts one from authentic knowledge. But this rejection of pseudo-erudition does not imply that knowledge is unnecessary: "Men who love wisdom must inquire into very many things."

Nor does wisdom consist in speculative construction. Reason is revealed in physical actuality. Heraclitus rejects the cosmic constructions of the Milesian philosophers. "Those things of which there is sight, hearing, and knowledge—these I honor most." He seems to be relapsing into vulgar empiricism when he says that the sun as it appears to us has the width of a human foot and that the sun is born anew each day. But perhaps such statements were merely intended to provoke. For elsewhere he doubts the value of sense perception: "The ears and eyes are poor witnesses to men if they have barbarian souls."

Knowledge is guided by something that is more than knowledge. "Most of what is divine escapes recognition through unbelief (*apistia*)." "If a man does not hope, he will not find the unhoped for, since there is no trail leading to it and no path." This is the import of the moving words: "A man's ethos (character) is his daimon," that is, not something that is merely given by nature, but something more. The daimon who guides me is not a strange being outside myself; it is myself as I authentically am, though I do not know myself as such.

All knowledge of *logos* and *nomos* is summed up in this one statement:

"If we are to speak with intelligence (*nous*), we must build our strength on that which is common to all, as the polis on the law, but even more so. All human laws are nourished by one, which is divine; for it governs as far as it will, and is sufficient for all, and then some."

3. Characterization. Heraclitus sees the *logos,* the unity of opposites, the flux of the world, the transcendent godhead; and he sees the possibility of man's ascent to wisdom.

The beginning of wisdom is not scientific inquiry, but the One, upon which everything depends; the philosopher's goal is not to know the world, but to put men on the right path.

Everything happens in accordance with the *logos.* It is hidden until the thinker reveals it. But Heraclitus does not ask why it is hidden, nor why there is a world in addition to the pure, peaceful fire, free from opposites, the ever-present source which is also eternal reason. An answer is provided in the Heraclitean tradition: Because of the opposition between satiety and need, all things come into being and pass away in an eternal cycle of world creation and world fire (*ekpyrōsis*). But this answer seems to conflict with Heraclitus' mode of thinking (and is not contained in any of the directly quoted fragments) for it extends the principle of opposition, which Heraclitus himself attributed only to the warring world, to the totality.

Heraclitean thinking is not a systematic construction but a vision formulated in maxims. His thinking is comprehensive, but revealed only in brief *aperçus.* It would be a mistake to look in Heraclitus for a construction of being, free from contradiction (and no philosopher who has attempted such a construction has ever succeeded). Confident in his profound insight, Heraclitus dispensed it in intermittent flashes of light.

He has only to ask and the answers are present. The questions are not developed; instead, the answers are proclaimed.

Heraclitus' ethos draws nourishment in thought from the ground of being, the *logos,* wisdom. Such thinking is a challenge. It strives to awaken, but counts on few, if any. Though the *logos* is common to all and can be made manifest, there is a tension between two conflicting tendencies in Heraclitus: he wishes to announce the *logos* to men, to make them aware of it and so to lead them to a better communal life; but at the same time, faced with the many who resist change, he resigns himself to solitary ineffectiveness, renouncing all hope of actualizing his vision of the *logos* except in the proud reality of his own life.

4. Influence. Heraclitus was in no way a founder; he did not establish a community, he addressed himself to all, to the few, to individuals, to no one. He was revered in antiquity but with the kind of respect that keeps its distance. There is an anecdote to the effect that Socrates, when questioned about Heraclitus by Euripides, replied: "What I have understood is ex-

cellent, and I am certain that what I have not understood is also excellent—
but it requires a Delian diver."

The Stoics cited the authority of Heraclitus. Hegel admired him. Karl
Marx's earliest work was devoted to him. Lassalle wrote a book about him.
Nietzsche praised him extravagantly.

Two of his ideas, the *logos* and the dialectic of opposites, have had an
extraordinary influence, though his name has not always been explicitly
related to them.

1. The principle of opposition has played an enormous role since Anaximander. It was taken up by the Pythagoreans and Parmenides. But only in
Heraclitus did it become the dominant form of thought. All Western dialectic goes back to Heraclitus and the successors of Parmenides. Heraclitus did
not systematically distinguish the modes of opposition; he lets them play side
by side and converge: contradiction, opposition, dichotomy, polarity, tension;
the whole–the part, unity–multiplicity, harmony–discord; life–death, waking–sleep, day–night. He did not differentiate the ways in which opposites
shift into one another, the modes of reversal, of dialectic movement in the
logical and in the real worlds. He expressed the notion of the opposites with
all the means at his disposal, including puns. Since Heraclitus touched upon
it in his universal vision, it has permeated the whole history of philosophy,
and to this day has not been elucidated in full systematic clarity.

In reference to Heraclitus, Aristotle wrote: Nature too seems to strive
toward the opposite; it produces harmony from opposites, not from likes:
for example, the male sex mates with the female. In painting, white is mixed
with black, yellow with red; in music high and low, long and short tones
are mingled to produce a unitary harmony; in the art of writing, vowels are
mingled with consonants.

Hegel claimed to have incorporated every one of Heraclitus' sayings in
his logic. And it is perfectly true that Hegel, with the help of the intervening
two thousand years of philosophical thought, developed his dialectic, or system of the categories of opposition, from what first made its appearance in the
thinking of Heraclitus.

2. The Stoics (beginning in the third century B.C.) interpreted the Heraclitean *logos* as all-pervading cosmic reason and fate. For Philo (c. 25 B.C. to
A.D. 50) the *logos* was the power of reason dwelling with God; it was the
first son of God, the second God, the mediator between God and man: the
word, God's eternal thought which created the world. In the Gospel of
St. John (second half of the first century) and from then on in Christian
theology the *logos* has been personalized as the incarnate word of God;
born into the world in Jesus, the *logos* is the second person of God.
Heraclitus had conceived the *logos* as a thought that opens the way to new
insights and extends man's horizons. In these historical transformations
it was objectivized, frozen into a philosophical doctrine.

PARMENIDES

Parmenides was a citizen of Elea, in southern Italy, at the turn of the sixth century B.C. He came of a wealthy and distinguished family. Some one hundred and thirty verses of his work in hexameters have been preserved.

The introduction to his poem relates the thinker's journey to the heavens: as a young man, he mounts the chariot of the sun maidens, who drive him from night to daylight, so swiftly that the axle "gave forth a pipe-like sound"; at the boundary between the two, they pass through a gate which Dikē opens for them, and he is led into the presence of the goddess, who receives him graciously. From her lips he learns the truth: "And now you must study all things: not only the unshaken heart of well-rounded truth (*alētheia*) but also mortals' opinions (*doxa*), in which there is no true reliance." Accordingly, the goddess' communication, and with it the poem, falls into two parts. Considerable fragments of the first part and a few reports concerning the second part have come down to us.

1. Being. The first fundamental idea is: "It is necessary to say and to think that being is, for it is possible for it to be, but it is not possible for 'nothing' to be." "Thou could'st not know that which is not nor utter it." "For never shall this be proved: that things that are not are." In terms of formal logic: being is or is not; its nonbeing, all nonbeing, is unthinkable; therefore being is and nonbeing is not.

Especially in the original Greek, these lines can either seem wonderfully meaningful or else startlingly empty. They bear witness to a profound emotion and yet they state only tautologies. For the first time in the West a thinker expresses his surprise that being is, that it is impossible to think that nothing is. His statement of what is most obvious is perfectly clear and at the same time supremely puzzling. Being is and nothing is not; this, for Parmenides, is a revelation of thinking through thinking.

The fundamental knowledge which sustains this philosopher's life—the actuality of being—is expressed in seemingly trivial sentences. Parmenides built a temple to the Pythagorean Ameinias, because through him he had found peace (*hesychia*)—in fundamental knowledge of the actuality of being.

It is futile to look in these sentences for a hidden meaning that might tell us more about being. Being cannot be expressed in terms of anything else; it can only be contemplated. Yet with Parmenides we can go further toward determining what this being is. For on this way, the true way (in contradistinction to the false way, which is to think nonbeing), many signs (*sēmata*) of being are disclosed. They follow necessarily from the process of thinking:

It is *unborn*. No origin can be found. "For what birth of it wilt thou look for? In what way and whence did it grow?" Not from any existing thing, for then there would be another, pre-existing being. Not from any non-existent thing, for then there would be no cause or necessity impelling it to spring sooner or later from nothingness and begin to grow. Only nothing can spring from nothingness. Hence being must either be whole or not at all. If it had been born at some time, it would not authentically be. Nor is it limited to the future. In it, rather, becoming and passing away are annulled. It is *imperishable*. It was not nor will be, "since it is now all at once, one, continuous."

Being is *one,* always identical, of equal power, cohesive. Being is inseparably close to being. It is not sometimes stronger and sometimes weaker; rather, it is everywhere wholly filled with being and indivisible. It is being (*on,* so first used by Parmenides), not a multiplicity of existing things (*onta,* as was said before Parmenides).

It is unique. For there is nothing and will be nothing outside of being.

It is whole. It is the extreme limit, hence complete on all sides. In other words, it is not something to be ended (thus it is not endless), or to be completed. It is comparable to a sphere. "It is immovable in the limits of its mighty bonds, without beginning or cessation. . . . The same and abiding in the same [place], it is set by itself, and thus it abides there firm and unmoved."

In Parmenides the signs (*sēmata*) of being are not images illustrating an abstract idea. Rather, they are what must necessarily be thought; when we think them, being itself is present. Thus Parmenides with his "signs" is not moving toward a sign language as later developed by mathematics and symbolic logic, but toward the cipher language peculiar to metaphysical speculation.

The emptiest thought carries the most enormous meaning. But as an empty thought that is quickly and easily mastered by the understanding, it remains an empty idea, without further meaning. Its meaning is expressed in the necessity of thinking the *sēmata,* for in this thinking the vision of being is re-enacted and the experience of peace in being is attained. Along with necessary contradiction and identity, the *sēmata* are images of thought not based on visual perception. Parmenides' fundamental statement is not an empty identity, but understood solely in its logical form, it is objectively empty. It is a thinking action which was possible in the naïveté (not primitivism) of creative beginning; it is still possible, though we cannot recapture the old candor. Logic and being merged, and both were unfolded in thought. Logic was not yet empty because it was not yet intended as logic. Accordingly, the vision is not a metaphor, but a necessary part of the thought. The tone of this thought is compounded of a compelling, imperious logic and of jubilant certainty in the ground of all things. The inexplicable is explained; the form is that of prophetic revelation.

Though being, that is, the knowledge that being is and must be and discloses certain signs, was for him an overwhelming emotional experience, Parmenides was obliged to think these signs in forms that were later termed categories. But his emotion also impelled him to devise *images analogous to mythical images:* Being is constrained by the Moira to be a whole and immovable. Overpowering necessity (*Ananke*) holds it within the bonds of the limit. Dikē does not relax the fetters of being, leaving it free to become or pass away, but holds it fast.

Parmenides' thinking experience of being is so powerful that it transforms the thinker. He enters into another "world," which is no longer world. He knows that *his* path leads "far from the path of mortals," and that to attain it through Themis and Dikē is a happy lot in contrast to the unhappy lot of ignorant mankind. The story of the journey to the heavens, from darkness into light, is not poetic ornament, but the sensuous, imaged form of the thought itself: truth is imparted, divine powers help lead the thinker to the goddess who communicates the pure truth; his own yearning for truth has itself this divine character. It is not a long, slow journey, but swift and sudden. The dividing line is the gate guarded by Dikē.

Image and thought can and must be seen in one. The poetry is not an external, artificial form, but the very essence of the thought. More than almost anywhere else, this thought must be understood in the form the philosopher gave it if it is to be understood at all.

Through reflection on being, Parmenides became aware that certainty of being has its origin in thinking: "Thinking and being are one and the same." And: "Thinking and that in respect of which it is thought are one and the same." "For you will not find thought apart from that which is, in respect of which it is uttered." Because our thought is necessary, what we think must be.

But this is not the thinking of common sense. Thought, we suppose, confronts being. But Parmenides distinguishes his thinking (authentic thinking in the *nous*) from the thinking that splits and differentiates: "Look at things which though far off are yet surely present to thought. For you cannot cut off being from holding fast to being." Thus in thought (the *nous*) being itself is present as a whole; the absent is also present.

The greatness of Parmenides' conception of being is lost if we attempt to put into it what is not truly his own. Measured by the logical richness of the differentiated categories or the perceptual richness of the world, Parmenides' being is so poor that it vanishes. For his boldly transcending thinking of this being is directed toward an imageless pre-categorial, or trans-categorial realm; yet transcendence in Parmenides is not somewhere else, it is wholly present. But this presence does not lie in the plenitude of the sensuous, temporal world. The radical distinction that gives Parmenides' thinking its power is between the seriousness of being and the trivial world of opinion.

Parmenides' "thinking" of "being" is clarified by contrasts:

In sharpest opposition to Anaximander's *apeiron,* this being is comparable to a sphere and is bound by limits (*peirata*). Being is not *apeiron* but *peras,* because it must be thinkable. What is thought is determined and therefore has limits. Only what can be understood through a logical operation carries the conviction of compelling thought. What being is, is thinkable. Only the thinkable is being. Thinking has become an absolute.

This also brings Parmenides into contrast with Heraclitus, whose *logos* is divine; mortals breathe it in and it becomes human thinking, a mere echo, not an absolute in itself.

2. *The world of appearance.* The counterpart to the fundamental thought, which is Parmenides' one and all, is the world of appearance. Nevertheless, he devotes considerable attention to it. The goddess first tells Parmenides the truth, then the false opinions of mortals. In the latter, Parmenides builds the world of appearance with the materials provided by traditional cosmology and traditional science, but contributes no new observations.

The genesis of the world and the genesis of false opinion (*doxa*) are the same. Illusion arose with the splitting of the one, which is linked to namegiving. Men named two appearances, light and darkness. They separated the ethereal fire and the lightless night, the one gentle, light, always identical with itself, the other dense and heavy.

But in this they erred. These are mere names, established in the language of deluded mortals who believe them to be true, as they believe of becoming and passing-away, being and nonbeing, change of place and variation of bright color, etc.: "Thus therefore, according to opinion, were these things created and are now, and shall hereafter grow and then come to an end. And from these things men have established a name as a distinguishing mark for each."

Few details of Parmenides' cosmology have come down to us. As in Anaximander, there were spheres occupied by fire, sun and moon, earth and life. But in the middle is the goddess who governs all. First she created Eros. Everywhere the goddess incites to mating. "Cruel birth and mating." But why is there not only the one truth? Why is there a world of appearance and not only being? We find no answer in Parmenides other than the description of the error. We can only construct an answer in the spirit of Parmenides: Appearance arises through being itself, which enters into a process of transformation and so gives rise to the modes of half-being—the being which is at the same time nonbeing, which, as we know, cannot be— and at the same time to the modes of appearance. Then the whole of being is lost, the absent is no longer present, the present is detached from the past and future. With the world of appearance, delusion is born.

Why, we may further ask, did Parmenides concern himself so much with the world of appearance? The goddess said to him in the beginning: "But nevertheless thou shalt learn these things (opinions) also, how one should go through all the things that seem, without exception, and test them." And when she has finished expounding the true doctrine of being, she repeats: "This disposition of things (*diakosmos*), all plausible, I tell thee; for so no mortal judgment shall ever outstrip thee." In view of the level and depth of Parmenides' thinking, it is inconceivable that he should set forth the science of illusion, anti-philosophy as it were, in order to be superior to men. What he actually does is to examine the world of appearance on the basis of its own necessity—that is, he surveys it and penetrates it from the standpoint of truth. *Doxa* must be thought in a way that is not identical with the thinking of wavering mortals. Philosophical thinking about the world of appearance must be above delusion, unfettered by appearance, finding, as it were, the truth of appearance in the ground of its unfolding; investigating appearance by means of a knowledge of appearance.

The fragments do not tell us how Parmenides related his view of appearance to his fundamental conception, but we find an indication in the reports of other writers. He not only taught that thinking and being are the same, but also held with the theorem, first made famous by Empedocles and often reiterated from Plotinus to Goethe, that like is perceived and known only through like. Thus Parmenides believed that for lack of fire the dead do not perceive light and warmth, but that they do perceive cold and silence. Everything that is has a knowledge (*gnōsis*). Man knows being with the *nous,* appearance with his mixed essence, and non-being when he is dead.

3. The decision. Parmenides demands decision (*krisis*) between the two ways, the way of truth (the thinking of being) and of error (the thinking of non-being). But since the thinking of nonbeing is impossible, he has no more to say about it. The great ubiquitous error, disastrous for all men, is a third possibility, halfness, the mixture of thinking of being and thinking of nothing. Those mortals who know nothing wander on this way, "two-headed, for perplexity guides the wandering thought in their breasts, and they are borne along, both deaf and blind, bemused, as undiscerning hordes, who have determined to believe that *it is and is not, the same and not the same,* and for whom there is a way of all things that turns back upon itself." Here Parmenides reduces the average man's opinion, lacking in self-awareness, to its essential meaning, or rather unmeaning, in formulas that are to be found in Heraclitus. (Scholars are in disagreement as to whether this passage is directed against Heraclitus himself; if it is, what more eloquent way of expressing contempt for Heraclitus than to interpret his formula, in which the older philosopher purports to state a world-shattering truth that the crowd fails to understand, as the opinion of this selfsame crowd, couched in clear language.) The goddess warns: Do not "let custom that comes of much experience force thee to cast along this way an aimless eye and a dreaming ear and tongue."

What Parmenides communicates as his own fundamental experience (at the very outset in the image and reality of the journey to the heavens), namely the transformation of his whole nature through his transformed consciousness of being, he now demands of all men and proclaims as the way of salvation. But it is typical of Parmenides as a philosopher, as a "knowing man," that this way should be opened up by compelling logical thought: "Judge by reasoning the much-debated proofs I utter."

4. The insoluble difficulties. The difficulties of this philosophizing do not reside in the fragmentary character of the tradition; they are rooted in the problem itself.

The sun maidens (divine powers) drive the young man in their chariot from the world of night to the world of light; and at the limit between the two, he is admitted by Dikē, who opens the gate. What is revealed to him within, the day, the light, pertains to the truth of being; what he has left behind him, the darkness, the night, pertains to opinion and appearance, that is, nonbeing. But in addition he learns that the difference between day and night is itself appearance. From out of the realm of appearance, remaining within appearance, he hears what makes even his ascent to the light illusory.

This difficulty stands at the very beginning of speculative philosophy: in the course of its operations, the philosopher's undertaking is destroyed by the very truth it attains. In arriving at truth, philosophy meets failure and vanishes. It speaks at the cost of departing from the truth it has already gained.

Or to put the same thing in a different way: if we think something, we must at the same time think something else, from which the first something differs or to which it is related. For Parmenides this thinking is the source of illusion through separation and name-giving. The truth must be thought as inseparably one, but in the thinking, differentiations are born. Parmenides thinks being, which is opposed to nothingness. But nothingness is unthinkable and, because it is illusory, should not be thought. Man is called upon to decide between two ways; this means that two ways have been differentiated and that both have been thought. But where a differentiation is made, it is not being that is thought; we are already in the realm of *doxa*.

In answer to this objection it is possible to argue: The opposition between being and nothingness is absolute. Once it is apprehended in thought, it ceases to be an opposition, for nothingness is not, only being is. With the true thought of the one perfect being, free from opposition, the other vanishes. If we take the true way, we perceive that it is the only way, that there is no other. Where Parmenides thinks being, there is no longer a decision. The imperative of transcending thought drives the thinker beyond opposition into the realm where there is no opposition.

Yet interpret as we will, the objection is not refuted. But far from destroying the philosophy, this only makes its meaning clearer. This meaning cannot be saved in the form of a compelling rational knowledge of something. Thus the objection is justified only when the philosophical meaning is abandoned. The philosophical meaning, in turn, can be acquired and preserved only at one with the thinker's thinking existence.

5. Influence. Parmenides' influence has been enormous. This may seem surprising in view of the predominantly logical character of his thinking. But for Parmenides the seeming emptiness of his statement was supreme fullness, and for all who came after him it represented a challenge to fill his molds of thought, which, once communicated, become purely formal.

But there are other reasons for his historical influence. The methods of thought he developed came to be utilized independently, while their original meaning was overshadowed or lost.

1. Parmenides wished by thought to gain a foothold beyond the origin of the world, which, under the name of *archē* (origin, principle), had already been conceived in a number of ways. However, his thought was interpreted *as a new approach to this very same* archē. Later thinkers tried to fulfill the demands raised by Parmenides' conception of being by reflecting on the origins as before, but now with the help of such *"sēmata"* of being as the elements (Empedocles), the infinitesimal, infinitely different particles (Anaxagoras), or the atoms (Democritus).

2. Parmenides did not formulate the axiom of contradiction, but he was first to apply it with a clarity that brings out the possibility of compelling thought through alternatives. Parmenides' aim was to permit being, eternal truth, to manifest itself, but his method became an instrument of compelling thought applicable to correct statements about anything whatever. From it developed logic and dialectics.

Thus what was originally a whole broke down into separate parts: first logic, which sets forth compelling formal relationships; secondly, metaphysical speculation, which looks upon itself as a methodical game that makes the profoundly serious communicable; thirdly, the aesthetic view of being and the world, the intellectual frivolity which traces an endless variety of figures of thought, none of them binding.

3. It was Parmenides who first explicitly stated that thinking is being, or being thinking. Only where this equation is recognized can we be certain that in pure thought we are not merely reflecting on a thought

content, not only effecting logical operations according to rules, but that thinking puts us into the very midst of being. Thought is the reality in which the whole of being is actualized as such. Being itself thinks.

Only when this thesis had been stated thus radically did it become possible to oppose it and to ask whether being and thinking must not, on the contrary, be conceived as separate if we are to discern the relation between them (it was Kant who first stated this position with full clarity). From this point of view, thought can no longer apprehend being, but can gain valid insight only into certain manifestations of being, which are accessible to it, while an intimation of being itself is conferred more by the failure of thought than by our thinking of any thought content. Thinking is no longer being, but a human activity oriented toward being. The idea that being itself is thinking becomes a cipher and ceases to be literal reality.

Parmenidean thinking became the nesting place of an attitude of thought rooted in faith. The thinkers of this type supposed that in cogent thought they possessed the bodily presence of being and in a valid idea the absolute truth. They concluded that this gave them the right to repress by violence any other thinking that might lay claim to truth. But when thinking becomes aware of its limits and of the diversity of its methods, the violence and fanaticism born of such an attitude disappear.

4. Parmenides operates with the inflections of the word "being." From the standpoint of subsequent logical and linguistic reflection, he employs the most universal form, the copula "is," which is present explicitly or implicitly in every statement. He uses the most universal category; for once it is thought, anything whatever is a mode of being. With Parmenides, the words which have always, before and since, been used unconsciously in all speech, took on special meanings: Greek: *estin, einai, onta, on, ousia;*—Latin: *est, esse, existentia, essentia;*—English: is, being, existent, existence, essence.

To consider only the universality of these words is to conceive them in their formal emptiness. They are indeed a factor in Parmenidean thinking, but the thinking itself, in this empty universality, has lost its meaning. For the instrument a thinker makes use of is not the whole of his thinking, least of all when the thinker is not even conscious of his instrument as an instrument, but in his very use of it is one with the substance of his thinking, as was the case in the magnificent innocence of the beginning. It is a paradox of speculation that what is emptiest can at the same time be most meaningful. When the essential meaning of "being," that most universal of words, resides not in its logical or linguistic form, but in an undefined emotion in the presence of all that is being, then the most abstract question about being becomes the most powerful.

For once the question was asked, nothing, nonbeing, made its appearance and from then on has left thinkers no peace. Parmenides said it was not thinkable and simply non-existent. Plato found that nonbeing could in a certain way be. The question of why being is and nothing is not attained its most penetrating formulation in Schelling: Why is there something and not nothing?

In order to fill out the thought of being, academic thinkers defined it and determined its fundamental modes. In the seventeenth century, after such thinking had been going on for two thousand years, it became known as ontology. Parmenides' thinking is the beginning of "ontology," but in the dogmatic, academic forms of ontology his provocative meaning was lost.

5. Parmenides does not call being God. But what he conceived as the signs of being, became a field of categories which were subsequently transferred to God when theologians sought to define His attributes. From Parmenides came the motifs appropriate to a thought structure embracing the imageless God, to the apprehending of transcendence by pure thought. His "ontology" provided "theology" with its tools.

6. The distinction betweeen truth and opinion, between the being of being and the illusion of the world, was later fixated in the so-called *theory of the two worlds*. This became possible once a certain independent reality was imputed to nature, i.e. the world of illusion, once illusion became a natural phenomenon, i.e. an appearance, while being became a transcendent realm, another being, a second world, a "world behind the world." With this the Parmenidean unity of being and knowledge was transformed into a dualism which, in a variety of forms, has run through all Western history.

Thanks to the radicalism of his propositions and the acuteness of his challenge, Parmenides was the great point of departure. Through him thought achieved self-awareness as an independent power; compelling in its conclusions, it unfolded its potentialities and so attained to the limits where thought incurs failure—a failure which Parmenides did not discern, but which he invited with the enormous demand he made upon thought.

In the *Theaetetus* Plato erected a monument to Parmenides, whom he regarded as the greatest of the pre-Socratic philosophers: "Parmenides is in my eyes, as Homer says, a 'revered and awe-inspiring' figure. I thought there was a sort of depth in him that was altogether noble. I am afraid we might not understand his words and still less follow the thought they express." Nietzsche, on the other hand, sensed the extraordinary in Parmenides and thought he understood it, but did not. He speaks of the "type of a prophet of the truth, who seems however to be made, not of fire but of ice," of "absolutely bloodless abstraction," of a "mind which logical rigidity has almost transformed into a thinking machine." Henceforth the truth would reside "only in the palest, most abstract generalities, in the empty husks of the vaguest words, as in a house of spider-webs."

COMPARISON BETWEEN
HERACLITUS AND PARMENIDES

1. *Their common situation.* Heraclitus and Parmenides were familiar with the thinking of their predecessors: the mythical thinking of Hesiod and the philosophical liberation from myth, the haphazard knowledge and the cosmological and cosmogonic constructions of the Milesians, the Pythagorean doctrine of the soul and transmigration, the monotheism of Xenophanes' "enlightenment"; they participated in the newly achieved independence of thinking, and knew Anaximander. They were in the same intellectual situation and both responded to an experience that had shaken the Greek mind. The new task they confronted presents an analogy to the powerful religious movements which rose at the same time, perhaps in connection with the Persian conquest of the Greek cities of Asia Minor. They sought peace in the thought of authentic being.

2. *The common new element in their thinking.* Essentially they achieved the same thing, but by different means: Parmenides with logical identity and the exclusion of the contradictory, Heraclitus with the dialectic that encompasses contradictions. Both were alive to the power of pure thought; their thinking is not determined by sense perception and concrete observation, which they used merely as a language in which to clothe their meaning. Always by rational means, both performed an operation that is not only rational. They discovered the possibility of a thinking that transcends all knowledge of the world, that looks into the world from somewhere else. They both looked upon this thinking as the absolute truth.

Both took great pains in the molding of their language, seeking simplicity and concentrating on the essential. This was the period of the severe "archaic" style in sculpture and of the beginnings of Attic tragedy.

Parmenides wrote epic hexameters, Heraclitus wrote prose in the manner of the ancient maxims of wisdom. The solemnity of Parmenides' poetry has its counterpart in the dignity of Heraclitus' prose. Within the traditional forms, both devised a new style. There had never been poetry like that of Parmenides. Even in form none of the older maxims equaled those of Heraclitus.

3. Agreement and opposition. In antiquity they were regarded as adversaries. Parmenides, it was said, teaches being, Heraclitus becoming. This sounds as though they had given opposite answers to the same question (what is the ground of all things?); as though one had said: it is being, forever identical and unchanging, and the other: it is eternal flux (*panta rhei*). Actually, both disclose being as well as becoming. Parmenides' being (*to on*) has its counterpart in the *logos* (or *to sophon* or the God) of Heraclitus; unborn, imperishable being in the always identical *logos;* Parmenides' distinction between truth and appearance in Heraclitus' hidden *logos.* Through insight (*noein*) Parmenides apprehends the whole of being at once, the absent is also present; with disciplined thinking (*phronein*) Heraclitus participates in the clash of opposites, in which the one *logos* is present and governs. The two thinkers' ideas are not mutually exclusive. Both think what eternally is, but in different, parallel ways. The one thinks being in logical identity, in the transcendent peace of always identical perfection, the other in logical dialectic, in the transcendent peace of the always identical law. The one finds the ground in identity, through which contradiction is destroyed, the other in contradiction, which is transcended in the unity of opposites. A conflict between the two becomes inevitable only if the claim of absoluteness is raised for their formulas.

They disclose, to be sure, very different casts of mind. In Heraclitus the accent is on separation in struggle, on the task of apprehending being in opposites, of finding peace through conflict, of gaining measure and discerning the law through thought. Parmenides dwells, from the outset, on the peace of always identical contemplation.

Did Heraclitus and Parmenides know each other and did the conflict between them help them to differentiate their ideas more sharply? Or was the elder merely combated by the younger? Or did they, though contemporaries, know nothing of one another? There is no sure answer to these questions. Even in our era with its highly developed communications, it is possible for two thinkers not to know each other. (Nietzsche never heard of Kierkegaard, who was thirty years his senior.) All we know with certainty is that Heraclitus and Parmenides lived at roughly the same time; the difference in their ages cannot have amounted to more than a decade or two. To our historical way of thinking, they are two independent but parallel thinkers, inseparably linked by their disagreements as much as by what they have in common. The character of their thinking becomes fully clear to us only when we consider them side by side.

4. Pure thought. Both move in the newly won area of pure thought. Measured by the standards of definite, empirical object thinking, such thinking is incomprehensible. Its statements seem to say nothing. Others have praised this mode of thinking, piously repeating its solemn figures, discern-

ing in it the "revealed face of necessity" or an "illumination of fate," or
maintaining that its vision of being confers peace or heroic endurance in
the face of suffering and disaster. While not entirely untrue, such statements
falsify the thought of Heraclitus and Parmenides by representing it as complete. For what began in this philosophizing can never be completed as an
objective possession and always remains to be completed in existential reality.
Perhaps such heroism and peace of mind had a higher reality in those thinkers than they have in the men of today. But their communication, as well
as their confirmation in thought, action, and day-to-day conduct, is a process that can never be concluded.

5. *Prophecy and will to power.* The personalities of both philosophers
share a trait that seems to exclude the possibility of taking the truth they
discovered as anything but a beginning, extraordinary to be sure, but in this
form unrepeatable and, above all, not exemplary. This common trait is their
prophetic self-certainty. Though they invoked not the authority of God, but
the force of their own insight, this insight was total and overpowering.
Parmenides puts it into the mouth of the goddess and Heraclitus, though
invoking no divinity, deposited his work in the temple of Artemis at Ephesus.
Both saw the source of their truth not in the voice of God but in the compelling power of thought. The essential is not obedience to a divine word, but
revelation through thinking. Having discovered the truth by their own resources, they felt far superior to other men. Favored with an unprecedented
insight, with an absolute certainty that made all further questions superfluous,
they took the attitude of intellectual tyrants. They knew their utterances to
be the language of being. Through their mouth spoke Truth itself, inspired
by the goddess (in Parmenides' image) or by all-pervading world reason
(in Heraclitus' conception). They saw an unbridgeable gulf between their
insight into the ground of things and the manner of thinking common to
other men. Thus, though their writings show a desire to convince and influence, they stood alone, beyond communication. They demanded obedience,
not friendship. They realized the form of existence of the solitary aristocratic
thinker, enhancing the aristocratic privilege conferred by right of birth
with the new claim to intellectual superiority. The self-sufficiency bestowed
by their certainty of being implied the right to dominate all others through
the truth which they alone had recognized.

Their attitude toward other thinkers was one of boundless arrogance.
Heraclitus cites many illustrious names, all with the most violent condem-
nation. Parmenides mentions no names, but seems to have disposed with
the utmost contempt even of Heraclitus (if Bernays is right) or of Anaximander (if Reich is right). Their work is permeated by exclusion, antago-
nism, a furious aggressiveness. There is a despotic spirit in both men.
With all the greatness of their insight, they failed to understand the nature
of such insight.

The seduction exercised by them is reflected in their influence on modern philosophy. Nietzsche's mimicry of pre-Socratic thinking, which led him to his inventive interpretations, culminated in a monstrous self-assurance (manifested, it is true, against the background of his mental illness and in no way detracting from his real greatness). We can look at it with awe and pity as on a unique historical phenomenon. But to imitate it today would be ludicrous, despicable, indeed impossible.

6. *Historical appraisal.* What preceded Heraclitus and Parmenides is for us historically interesting and emotionally stirring because it gives us a glimpse of ancient ways of thinking, but the content, in so far as it is known to us, belongs to the dead past. It is Heraclitus and Parmenides who gave us the first texts with which we can still directly philosophize. With their simplicity, they arouse inexhaustible thought. The elucidation of their meaning confronts us as an endless task. Here we find propositions that are as actual and timeless as only great philosophy can be.

Nevertheless, these two, the earliest philosophers whose writings still exert an influence, can also mislead. Whereas Anaximander brought about a revolutionary upheaval in man's thinking attitude toward things and examined all the possibilities with universal openness, these two limited their scope to metaphysics which they proclaimed to be the only true knowledge. In so doing, they succumbed to a new prejudice, magnificent in its way but dangerous. For though their speculation was deeper and clearer than any that preceded it, even that of Anaximander, they showed nothing but incomprehension and contempt for all the thought which, by virtue of its intellectual weight and creative potentialities, was pregnant with the future, condemning it as pseudo-knowledge or false erudition, fortunately for us, in vain. For in our temporal existence the only way to follow the marvelous paths that Heraclitus and Parmenides pointed out is to assume the tasks of mankind and not haughtily to brush aside the realms of politics and science and close our eyes to the world.

PLOTINUS

I. LIFE AND WORKS

Plotinus (c. 203–270) lived amid the collapse of ancient civilization in a period of transition when the beauty of the ancient world knew a last flowering before entering the era of late antiquity, soon to be inaugurated by Diocletian and Constantine.

We do not know exactly where Plotinus was born, nor have we any inkling of his ethnic and social origins. He himself never mentioned his parents or childhood. The report that he was born in Lycopolis, Egypt, did not make its appearance until long after his death. The name Plotinus is Roman; he spoke and wrote Greek, "often making mistakes in pronunciation."

At the age of twenty-eight he was drawn to Alexandria by his interest in philosophy, but was dissatisfied until he heard Ammonios Saccas. "This was the man I was looking for," he declared after the first lecture, and stayed with him for eleven years. When thirty-nine, he took part in the Emperor Gordianus' Eastern campaign in order to familiarize himself with Indian wisdom. At the age of forty—when Philip "the Arabian" was Emperor—he went to Rome, where he organized conferences at which philosophical texts were read and discussed, and gathered students and supporters. "When he was speaking, his intellect visibly illuminated his face, a slight moisture gathered on his forehead. He spoke with fervid inspiration. . . . He was far removed from Sophist grandiloquence, his delivery suggested friendly conversation."

Plotinus "seemed ashamed of being in the body." When Amelius wished to paint his portrait, he declined with the words: "Is it not enough to carry about this image in which nature has enclosed us? Do you really think I must also consent to leave, as a desirable spectacle to posterity, an image of the image?"

He lived in Rome for twenty-six years, had wealthy friends whose estates he was free to visit, was on friendly terms with the Emperor Gallienus and his empress Salonina. Under their auspices a city of philosophers—Platonopolis—was to be established in Campania, under the direction of Plotinus, but the project was not carried out. Distinguished men and women on the point of death brought him their children to educate and entrusted him with their fortunes to administer. "Consequently, his house was full of boys and girls." He was called upon as an arbiter in quarrels, but never had an enemy.

In 268 Plotinus' situation changed completely. After the murder of Emperor Gallienus, his school disintegrated. Some of his most important disciples left Rome. Long a sufferer from leprosy, Plotinus fell mortally ill. He grew hoarse and blind, his hands and feet festered. His remaining students avoided him, "since he still insisted on greeting everyone at close quarters." He was isolated on the estate of his friend Zethos in Campania. Only his physician went to see him. He attached little importance to the care of his body. He died two years after Gallienus at the age of sixty-six.

Even Porphyry, in his biography, tells strange stories about Plotinus, recalling the lives of the saints: he possessed a superior knowledge of spirits. He could identify a thief in a crowd. He could predict what would happen to young men in later life. A certain Olympius attempted by the use of magical formulas to bring down the harmful influence of the stars on Plotinus. Plotinus saw what was happening and the harm fell on Olympius. An Egyptian priest decided to conjure up Plotinus' daimon in the temple of Isis. "When the daimon was called, a god appeared. Happy art thou," said the Egyptian, "who hast a god for a daimon and no guardian spirit of low degree." A friend came to see Plotinus on his deathbed. When Plotinus told him he would try to make his "divine-in-us" rise up to the divine-in-the-universe, a snake glided under the bed and disappeared into a hole in the wall. Plotinus was dead. (The snake was one of the forms taken by the soul as it left the room of one who had just died.) Plotinus' own writings show that he was utterly indifferent to magic. But soon after his death his philosophy was appropriated by magical and theurgic sects, who wove such legends into his biography.

The work: Plotinus and two other disciples were said to have pledged themselves to keep the teachings of Ammonios secret. The others had broken silence. It was only late in life, at the age of forty-nine, that Plotinus, in response to the urgent pleas of his students, began to write. After his death, Porphyry collected his work. He divided it into six groups of nine treatises (*Enneads*). The whole work was written during a period of seventeen years. According to Porphyry, the chronological order is established for some of the groups.

Some of the writings are didactic treatises, others are brief lectures; some seem carefully constructed, others are long critical exchanges; some are vivid descriptions of intellectual visions, others ask question upon question, present possibilities, and leave almost everything undecided. This "inquiring" style also expresses meditative action, the presence of the thinking soul in the realm of the essential. The same metaphysical mood pervades all the writings. Not infrequently the style takes on a note of religious solemnity. In addressing the logical faculty of speculative insight, Plotinus adjures the soul to remember its eternal home. He deals with experience, the contemplation of the beautiful, freedom of action, the movement of dialectical thinking, and finally, incommunicable ecstatic union with the One. His truth lies not in the abstractions of a schema, but in the power of concrete discussion. He wrote as he thought (Bréhier) and must have spoken as he wrote. Hence the unusual persuasiveness of the texts.

Porphyry tells us that once Plotinus "had worked out his design mentally from first to last . . . he wrote out at one jet all he had stored in his mind, as though copying from a book. He never looked over what he had written— his sight did not allow of it. His handwriting was slovenly; he misjoined his words and cared nothing for spelling; his one concern was for the idea." This manner of writing makes philological reconstruction extremely difficult.

The form of Plotinus' communication is in keeping with the content of his philosophizing. He never wrote a "system of philosophy." In a wealth of detailed analyses he repeats the whole over and over, in different contexts.

II. DESCRIPTION OF THE PLOTINIAN "SYSTEM"

It will be useful at the outset to draw up a schema of the whole structure. This schema recurs in nearly all the writings, though it is not the essential. A knowledge of it will help us to understand Plotinus' basic philosophical acts:

A. *Matter and the One:* The world is being. It is not self-grounded but is an intermediate being between Above-Being and nonbeing.

Above-Being, the supreme, is unthinkable and hence ineffable. Plotinus calls it the One, but goes on to say that it is neither the number one, nor the one as contrasted with the other, nor the unity of a multiplicity, but the One which as such cannot be thought, for any attempt to think the One produces duality and multiplicity.

Nonbeing is matter. Like Above-Being, it cannot be thought. Thus both have the same negative attributes: they are undetermined, formless, without quality and without quantity. They enter into no category. But in contrast to the Supreme One, the nonbeing of matter is not only without measure and limit, but also unstable, passive, and always deficient. It is utterly poor. The lowest level (*bathos*) of every single existence is matter and is utterly dark.

Being emanates from Above-Being but is contingent on nonbeing. Originating in the One, the stream of existence flows downward, engendering descending stages of being culminating in nonbeing. All beings are because there is nonbeing; in order to be, they must contain nonbeing. Although matter is not, it is not nothing. In so far as it is, it is the falsehood of non-being, which is present in everything that is.

B. *The scale of beings:* The scale of beings extends from the Above-Being of the One to the nonbeing of matter; in its center is the soul. The soul looks upward toward the One through the intermediary of the *nous* (the spirit, the intelligible world of pure forms) and downward toward matter through the intermediary of nature (the corporeal world). Thus there are five descending principles: the One, the spirit, the soul, nature, matter. Being embraces the three middle stages: spirit, soul, nature.

In the looking-upward of rational insight, the soul sees the timeless, self-sufficient world of forms, which taken together constitute a closed totality (the cosmos of the spirit). These forms are called Ideas. They are the archetypes of all existing things, and as such they are true Being, while everything that comes after them is a mere copy, having only apparent Being.

In its looking-downward, the soul becomes the world-soul which gives life to nature as a whole, while individual souls give living unity to all the many beings. Entering into nature, which is spatial and temporal, the souls become in part spatial and temporal. But in their true Being they are above nature, timeless and immortal. In the course of natural existence, the soul is wrapped in veils and ultimately, in its lowest descent, is hidden from itself, but its innermost essence remains indestructible.

C. *The categories:* Objective Being consists of the two remaining stages, the intelligible world and the sensory world (spirit and nature) which are known to us through their categories. As an intermediate link, the soul has no categories of its own. It is and knows only in terms of the two other worlds above and below it. It knows the realm of the spirit through the intelligible categories: Being, identity, difference, motion and rest (taken from Plato's *Sophist*); it knows the realm of nature through the sensory categories: space, time, quality, quantity, etc. (the categories of Aristotle). Matter and the One, however, cannot be encompassed in categories, for they are beyond thought.

Where existence is conceived in stages, there is a tendency to intercalate more and more stages. This is what happened in later Neoplatonic thinking with its endlessly expanding "geography" of spheres, realms, and powers. But Plotinus states expressly that there are three and only three hypostases: the One, the spirit, and the soul. Nature plays no part in his meditation on authentic being. Natural phenomena are of no interest to him. Matter is merely the ultimate limit of the emanations of the One.

Thus for Plotinus there are not two powers as in dualistic doctrines. Light and darkness, spirit and matter, good and evil are not two independent, conflicting principles. In Plotinus' thinking of the One and the Other, matter is the counterpart of the *logos* of spirit, not of the Supreme One. For Plotinus there is only the One, whence beings are engendered and to which they return in an eternal process.

D. *Spirit, soul, nature* are the three intermediate realms, the realms of being.

Though the one is above it, the spirit (*nous*) is true being. It is the timeless life of the pure forms (archetypes or ideas). It is thought; therefore in the spirit thinking and the object it confronts coincide; thinking and Being become identical. The spirit does not think an Idea as something alien, but as itself. It is self-consciousness. But since this self-thinking implies a cleavage between thinking and its object, the spirit contains both the One and the Other: the spirit is unity in multiplicity.

The spirit is praised as the most beautiful of all things. It dwells in pure light. It embraces all being, of which the beautiful world of nature is only a shadow. There is nothing unspiritual, dark, or unmeasured in it. It leads a life of bliss.

The soul is a copy and product of the *nous*. In looking up at the *nous,* the soul engenders nature, the cosmos. It is the creator of the world, the animating principle of the temporal world, but itself immaterial and indivisible. As world-soul, it is eternal and majestically at rest. As individual soul, it inhabits astral gods, demons, men, animals, and plants. The world-soul, which is also the soul that inhabits the astral gods, is immortal. For it links beginning and end in rotary motion to form an eternal present. The other individual souls contain a mortal and an immortal part. Having taken on the husks of finite, temporal existence, which is perpetually coming into being and passing away, they too are mortal.

In the soul everything is present, nature in its perception, the *nous* in its thinking, the One in the dialectical transcending of all thought and in ecstasy. But matter is present in not-seeing and not-thinking; when we peer into the darkness of night, our seeing is a not-seeing.

Nature is the sensuous world situated in space and time, the corporeal world that can be seen, heard, and touched. It is not matter, which is incorporeal, imperceptible, and unthinkable. Substances and bodies are matter that has been already formed and so drawn into being.

Nature owes its existence in part to the eye of the soul and is itself an unconscious seeing—for its innumerable living forms are permeated by the *logos* of the soul. Thus, though nature is without representations or concepts, it sees into itself. It creates like an artist in accordance with ideas, but without conscious images. The things and beings of nature are the product of this silent seeing. It creates as a geometer draws figures, but it does not design, the bodies take shape of their own accord. Its consciousness is that of a sleeper: nature is a sleeping soul. This soul has brought forth, and breathed life into, all the beings of the land and sea and air, as well as the sun and the divine luminaries of heaven.

Individual things come into being and pass away according as the soul gives them life or departs from them. But the world as a whole does not cease, because the spirit and the world-soul shine forever.

E. *Descent and ascent:* The question now arises: Why this descent from the One? Why are the spirit, the soul, nature, matter? Plotinus' answers, though abounding in formulations of the problem, offer no solution.

The One is motionless and self-sufficient. If there is a second something after it, it must come into being without any will or motion on the part of the One. What comes after the One is an unwilled consequence. Those who say that "the Creator decided at some time to bring it forth" are mistaken. The "copy" has existed as long as the "archetype." In Plotinus there is no Platonic demiurge who produces the world from matter while contemplating the Ideas, nor a Biblical God who creates it from nothing, nor does the world develop from eternal potentialities as in Aristotle. In Plotinus the world comes into being by a process that was later termed emanation. He himself had no concept for it, but merely set forth the mystery in countless images:

The Other is like a radiance bursting forth from the One, like the light surrounding the sun, or the heat radiated by fire, or the cold given off by a lump of ice, or the fragrance shed by a perfume. The greater the distance from the One, the weaker becomes the light, until it loses itself in darkness, emptiness, nothingness.

In another image, the universe flows from a source which feeds rivers but never runs dry. Or it is like the life of a great tree, which pervades the whole, though its principle remains concentrated in the root and is not dispersed. Or the One is compared to the center around which a circle moves.

Other metaphors are based on generation, vision, and love: generation is not a creation from nothing, or a fashioning out of some material, but the mysterious process of transmitting life—the product is no less an independent being than is its source. A son is not an artifact depending for its existence on its maker; he is an independent self, yet it was not himself but his father who brought him into being. Plotinus calls the One the father, the *nous* the son, and the world-soul the grandson. But generation comes to pass through vision. All Being is a product of seeing. Thus the One engenders the *nous*. Standing still in order to see, it becomes *nous* and enters into being. Looking upon the earlier stage as a prototype, each stage engenders its copy in the following stage which sees in turn, vision engendered by vision, and carries on the cycle. Descent-generation and upward contemplation are two aspects of the same process. To see is to love. The lovers are the seers who strive toward the Ideas. Even the animals, in procreating, are moved by the unconscious concepts within them. Generation, the act of vision, is a drive to create many forms, to fill the universe. But every begotten creature yearns toward the begetter and loves him.

Because the One is perfect, without need or desire, it overflowed and so brought forth the world. But in overflowing the One incurred no loss (like the sun, which remains unchanged despite the rays it sends forth). Nor is any stage diminished in producing the next after it.

In every stage, however, the begetter is simpler and better than the begotten. The principle does not need what follows it, but the product needs the principle. Nothing is subtracted from the higher, preceding stage. Why must the begotten be inferior to the begetter? It might be argued that, on the contrary, the product can grow and become better, that generation tends not downward but upward. Plotinus does not ask this question. But in all his metaphors he gives us the answer. The light is inferior to its source.

Each transition from stage to stage has a character of its own. The One is self-contained, eternally at rest, but something happens "around it." How so?

The One is not spirit, is not "an intellectual Principle; how then does it engender an intellectual principle? Simply by the fact that in its self-quest, it has vision: this very seeing is the intellectual principle." The spirit should not be derived from the One, but from the spirit itself. Thinking, the spirit "begins as one, yet does not remain as it began, but unawares, as though drunk with sleep, becomes many. It unfolds, because it wants to possess all things."

From the *nous* the next step is to the world-soul and to nature. Looking upon the archetypes in the Ideas of the *nous,* the world-soul engenders the world without plan or activity, without sound or effort. Nothing escapes it. Perpetually it regains its domination over conflicting things. For it is always the All.

Plotinus conceives the process as necessary. What sort of necessity is this? Plotinus replies: It was impossible that the All should remain at rest in the intelligible as long as something other could come into being in the hierarchy of things. Every stage engenders the stage below it. Only matter, because it is without energy, engenders no ensuing stage. In achieving maturity and fulfillment, all beings engender something other, for they are not content to remain within themselves. So it is with the One. For "how could the most perfect remain self-set—the first good . . . how could it grudge or be powerless to give of itself?"

Like all Plotinus' images and concepts, his notion of being as an unwilled product of the Supreme One, which it is impelled by necessity to engender, aims at something that cannot be attained in any image or concept. What he has in mind is not a necessity superior to the One. For such a necessity would be the source, more powerful than the Supreme One.

To each step downward in the generative process, there corresponds an ascending movement: the contemplation of the higher stage, the love of the begotten for the begetter.

But are all the lower stages in this ascending movement surpassed and negated for the benefit of the highest? Does Plotinus hold that in the end, when the fall is reversed and evil overcome, the One will stand all alone in infinite bliss and self-sufficiency? Not at all. If Above-Being were all alone, the world would have remained within it, hidden and formless; there would be no beings.

Thus the world is a place of transition, situated at once in light and darkness. It is beautiful and divine, because it originates in the One. It is a shadow, a reflection, incomplete and full of failings, because it is everywhere vitiated by orderless matter, the untruth of nonbeing. In so far as Being is formed, it is beauty, truth, the good; but in so far as every existent, even the best, contains a vestige of unformed matter, it partakes of ugliness, untruth, and evil.

Hence in Plotinus both are possible and true: love of the world's Being in all its stages, as a revelation and reflection of the One (which in its superabundance cannot but overflow), and the yearning to be free from the world, to return from existence, considered as a shadow distorted by the nonbeing of matter, to true Being and beyond it to the One, to cast off the veil of illusion and become fullness of Being. (It would have been better, says Plotinus, if the spirit had not unfolded its self; for in this unfolding, the One was followed by the second, which ushered in the whole hierarchy of stages and the cycle of the world.)

When Plotinus' thinking is thus set forth as a "system," it produces the effect of a story in concepts and images. But in the presence of these logical relations and illustrative metaphors, one wonders: how does he know all this? Nowhere is there an empirical or logical derivation from a source. Is he, then, not merely spinning out fairy tales that bring no insight? The system is pure invention and might have taken an entirely different form.

The first reply to such criticism is that any such exposition of Plotinus' system is in itself a distortion. His writings contain no such rounded picture. We find the formulations, but always in different contexts and modulations. Plotinus himself points the way to true philosophical insight as follows:

We should *dwell* where the One is present, which is none of all that which comes after it; we should marvel and rest and behold. We should perceive it in the things that are after it, its reflection.

We should *pray*. Asked why the One did not remain within itself and how being grew from it, Plotinus says: "We should speak of it by invoking God, by extending our soul in prayer when we alone confront Him alone." This has been interpreted as meaning that Plotinus prayed God to grant him insight. Not at all. He does not pray for anything; it is in prayer itself, alone with the One, that he hopes to gain the *presence* which can enable a man to speak meaningfully of the Supreme. This way of knowledge does not begin with a theorem from which corollaries are derived, but with a vision which remains its sole source and goal. It does not select an object to be examined, but in the objective world of appearances finds a fullness that transcends subject and object.

Plotinus teaches us to make our way through representations that are transcended, to attain, through the things of the world, to that which is not an object. "Call on God . . . and pray Him to enter. And may He come bringing His own universe with all the gods that dwell in it." We speak of the One, but we do not utter it. We do not have it by knowledge, but we are not entirely without it.

He tells us to start from the *experience of our own reality*. "Even when we call the One the cause, we are saying nothing of the One itself; we are merely affirming something that comes to us, for something comes to us from it, whereas the One is self-enclosed. We who circle around it, so to speak, from outside, may only interpret our own experience, as we alternately approach it and fall away from it." "To the best of our ability, we characterize it (the One), by something similar in ourselves. For in us, too, there is something of it, or rather, there is no point at which it is not, for those to whom it is granted to partake of it." In applying concepts to the One, "we say nothing about the One itself, but seek merely to make it as intelligible as we can to ourselves." We speak of the workings of the One after the manner of mystics, who "know that they have something higher within them, but do not know what it is."

This experience which Plotinus takes as his starting point cannot be described as a psychological phenomenon; it draws all its light from objectifying thoughts that do not attain the goal of their quest but circle around it, deriving their meaning from it alone. This is not a psychological knowledge of experiences or states, but an illumination of myself, the thinker, in so far as I am in the realm of Being.

Here Plotinus presents a parallel to other thinkers with fundamentally different positions. Plotinus does not know the One but his own experience, which in a certain measure shares in the One; Luther rejects the *theologia gloriae* (objective knowledge of God) in favor of the *theologia crucis* (God's revelation, which shows us the way to Him); Kant perceives the emptiness of all metaphysical knowledge and gives our knowledge of the intelligible new depth through free action.

Plotinus' point of departure explains the *methods* employed in the philosophical acts which we shall now retrace in attempting to understand the content of his thinking:

1. Plotinus carries out operations of thought which transcend all definite objects and every tangible form: from the multiplicity of beings to the one Being, from many gods to God, from the spirit to its source, from the intelligible to the unintelligible, from Being to Above-Being. Every being and everything that is thinkable is transcended in a movement toward that which is above and before it (toward the *epekeina pantōn*).

2. This transcending is effected in a series of stages. The goal, an ineffable ultimate experience, is always present as a point of reference. It is called union with the One. In it culminate all the stages of knowledge.

3. The total process of transcending is composed of speculative operations, all fundamentally the same but varied according to a wide range of categories. From life the eye is directed toward the true life, from forms to the eternal forms, from motions to the first motion, from the many beautiful things to beauty as such. Oriented by what is accessible, the way leads toward that which is in principle inaccessible. Much use is made of metaphors, images pointing to the archetype. "From the way the shadow of the Good appears we must conceive what its archetype is like." As we approach the cosmos of the spirit, we find this shadow playing around it. And once we have "beheld the cosmos of the spirit (we) must inquire after the Creator who has begotten so glorious a son."

4. In all the methods a single impulse is at work: the soul's drive toward its source, which it finds in contemplation and love; in the recollection of its origin; in self-purification. To attain this source is the soul's greatest joy. It confronts two possibilities: ascent or further fall. Philosophical thinking elucidates the alternative, showing the way and filling the soul with beatitude, the loving vision of knowledge.

The instrument (but also the symbol) of this whole manner of thinking is the systematic view of the universe outlined in our schema. In principle it is always the same, though represented in many different ways. It provides a frame for the various operations deriving from the traditional modes of speculation.

In this philosophizing purely rational evidence is not yet the criterion of truth. Wherever we stand, we look upward in love and yearning to something higher. Here we have an absolute consciousness, certain of itself, seeking enlightenment through self-understanding, not the explanation of one thing by another. Accordingly, we cannot find the truth of such thinking by logical operations or objective experience, which are merely its medium, but only in our own Existenz; we agree or disagree in so far as we perceive our own existential potentialities in it. In either case our understanding of it comprises a self-understanding. Without this existential testing of its truth, a purely objective or historical exposition of Plotinus' thinking must remain hopelessly alien from it, providing no contact or the slightest glimmer of understanding.

III. TRANSCENDING AS A WHOLE

For Plotinus as for Plato the process of transcending consists of two steps. The first transcends sense perception and attains to that which cannot be seen but only thought. A visible triangle is never exactly identical with the triangle of thought. Mathematical truth applies to the objects of an ideal world. But this ideal world encompasses more than mathematical forms, namely everything thinkable, everything that exists in thought. This ideal world of necessary thoughts is the infinite world of archetypes, of which the sensuous world discloses infinite copies.

Both the sensuous and the spiritual world are immanent; both are within the range of man's perceiving and thinking. The first transcending step from the perceptible to the intelligible, to that which can only be thought, merely provides the starting point for the second step, in which not only the visible is transcended, but the thinkable as well. In the world of the thinkable Plotinus still finds no rest, but goes on to search for its ground, its source. But this question cannot be answered by determinate thought. Anything we can think belongs to the intellectual world we are trying to transcend. Thinking, we take a step which is no longer thought, for as thought it cannot stand up against the proposition that the existence of the unthinkable is thinkable. Thinking presses to the limit that it cannot transcend but, in thinking this limit, spurs us to pass beyond it.

What is Plotinus' goal? The unthinkable. "It is called the First, because it is simpler and without need, because it is not manifold. . . . It is uncontained. . . . If then it neither originates in another, nor is any sort of composition, nothing can be above it." It is called the One. It is called the Good. The soul strives toward it: "And as long as there is something that is higher than what is present, (the soul) strives upward, but it cannot rise above the Good."

The aim of this transcending is named: the First, the One, the Good. But it is not what these words mean. And so Plotinus enjoins us: "Proceed thus: if you say 'The Good,' add nothing in your thought: for if you add something, you will diminish it by as much as you add." That is to say: to name it does not make it thinkable. The mere statement "that it is One, is false." Any notion that the unthinkable might be thought must be dispelled by negative statements. It is described as needing nothing, possessing nothing, supremely independent, existing for itself, unalloyed, removed from all contingency and association. All these are negative statements, they say what it is not. It is not being, not any existing thing, not thought, not self-awareness, not life, not motion. Whatever we can think, we must say: it is not this.

Over and over again Plotinus enjoins us: Take away all other things when you wish to speak of the One or to achieve awareness of it. And when you have taken everything away, do not try to add something to it but ask whether there might be something that you have not yet taken away from it in your thinking. Even Being is imputed to it only "under the pressure of words." Strictly speaking, we may not call it "this" or "that." It is not different from something other, and there are no differentiations within it. It does not think, it is not mind, for, since it is unwanting and related to nothing outside it, it has no need to think; nor does it think itself, for in it there is no differentiation or multiplicity, hence it has no self-consciousness. However—and this is all-important—what is not thought in thinking must not be interpreted as nothingness but rather as superabundance.

For we are always repelled by the negative. "Should we," asks Plotinus, "grow sceptical and suspect that it is *nothingness?*" And he answers: "Assuredly it is none of the things whose primal source it is." The only reason why it cannot be said to be being, or thinking, or life is that it is above all these. It is what it is not, not because it is less, but because it is more than what it is not. Thus Plotinus turns the "not" into a positive. Because the One is more, it encompasses and does not exclude what it is not. "Yet it is not unconscious, for all contents are in it . . . there is life in it . . . it is a thinking turned upon itself, a kind of self-awareness; it signifies a thinking in eternal immobility—different from the thinking of the intellect." Its nonbeing is a superabundance: "The giver is not necessarily identical with what he gives: . . . the giver is the higher, the given the lesser. . . . If spirit is life, the giver has given life, but he himself is more beautiful and of higher value than life . . . the life of the spirit is his reflection, not his life."

What cannot be thought can also not be said. Thus discourse concerning the unthinkable One is a perpetual saying and unsaying. To call it the absolutely other is to inject the category of difference into it; in being thought, the transcendent is reduced to immanence. Thus such turns of speech as: it is outside of all categories; it is "beyond all things," "it is entirely different"; it is "more than" or "above"; it is the completion of all things— all must be unsaid. Such locutions serve a purpose in the operation of transcending, but in the end they must be dropped because of their inadequacy.

One way in which Plotinus unsays such statements is to point out that what is said of the One does not apply to the One itself but only to the One in relation to us, not to the One as such but from our point of view. "It is not good for itself; it is the good for other things." When we "call it the cause, we are not saying what it does, but what is done to us." Here the cause is not a cause, but only seems so from the standpoint of the effect. The relation of the One to us is not a relation, but only appears to be from our point of view. Yet this unsaying is itself unsaid, for Plotinus speaks most emphatically of the One as that "from out of which everything else is and lives." "All beings yearn for it, as though suspecting that without it they could not be."

In speaking of the One Plotinus, carried away by enthusiasm, speaks from the depths of his soul, but in so doing renounces the possibility of knowledge. His imagination is inexhaustible in paradoxes: The First loses nothing, since the cause does not dissolve in the effect—it causes things to become but need not—it overflows but loses none of its fullness. The One perseveres in perfect rest and does not look down to what comes after it. It would be all the same to the First if there had been no second. It remains undivided, loses nothing, and wants for nothing. But that which has become turns to it and looks upon it and is filled with it.

How differently Plotinus' thinking appears to us when we describe it objectively as a system of the universe, and when we participate in the transcending thought itself. Only in the actual progress of the ideas and actualizations is the basic riddle of existence disclosed in the Plotinian manner, but never is an answer found that can stand as a content of knowledge.

Plotinus also calls the One, the ultimate transcendence, *God*. Everything visible, everything thinkable, everything we are and can apprehend becomes subordinate to the godhead. This transcending of all immanence, all glory and greatness in the world and of all spirit toward the divine is by no means self-evident, much less the radicalism with which, in Plotinus, transcendence is safeguarded against any attempt to think it, to bring it closer, to touch or embody it. There is nothing self-evident about ascribing all depth and power to this transcendence and making it the one and only center.

But God in Plotinus is also called the cosmos of the spirit (*nous*) and the world-soul; the heavenly bodies are gods, and there are also the demons that fill the atmosphere. In accordance with the Greek tradition, Plotinus imputes multiplicity to the divine. Transcending takes place within the divine as within all being. And only in this transcending is Plotinus enraptured by that which is the goal of all his thinking, but which he cannot think or utter and for which "God" is only one name among many. This name, however, is not expressly unsaid, although this godhead cannot be considered on the same level as all the many gods. No philosopher has lived more in the One than Plotinus. But his One is not the living God of the Bible, it is not moved by anger, is not a bringer of mercy and redemption. Plotinus' God is infinitely loved but does not love in return. Everything is through Him, but not by virtue of His will. This one God has no cult and no congregation. The soul takes flight with the One-in-it to the Only-One. The godhead is reached by means of an ethical life and, in philosophizing, through a speculative dialectic that forbids all intelligible, and *a fortiori* sensuous, fixation. Prayer is a philosophizing self-movement toward God.

For us everything depends on God, on the One: "We are in higher degree when we move toward him; to be far from Him signifies a lower degree of being." Life on earth is homelessness, exile. But this God is not a personal being who turns to us in love. "The Godhead does not yearn for us as though it existed for us; we yearn for it, we exist for it." Like many of the great philosophers (Aristotle, Spinoza), Plotinus recognizes no love of God for man, but only the love of man for God, which is the foundation of all authentic life.

IV. THE STAGES OF KNOWLEDGE

The process of transcending toward that which cannot be transcended passes through the stages of knowledge. Plotinus distinguishes perception (*aisthēsis*), understanding (*logismos*), and reason (*nous*). Perception comes before thought. Understanding achieves knowledge in differentiation, by proofs, inferences, and reflection; its knowledge is indirect. Reason sees the unity of what has been differentiated, the One in the many, immediately and without reflection. What lies beyond these three stages no longer partakes of thought, it is more than thought; namely, union with the One; every object vanishes and I myself with it; filled with the ground of all being, both become one with it.

Thus thought occupies an intermediate position between Less-than-thought and More-than-thought. What is thinking? It is a process which distinguishes between itself and the object of thought and between one object and another. Thought implies diversity.

In this intermediate sphere between sense perception and the unity beyond thought Plotinus distinguishes mere understanding and reason, spirit (*nous*). The understanding operates indirectly, through reflections and inferences, it makes things with tools. Reason, on the other hand, beholds: it has immediate vision of the One in the many. As the Egyptians see the thing itself in the hieroglyph, so vision apprehends its objects, not by discursive thinking, but in a single act. In bringing forth the universe the Creator does not think out one thing after another like an artisan making things with his hands and with tools, but produces the whole at one stroke. Such is the nature of man's vision when, transcending thought, he apprehends the essence of things.

But—and this is crucial for Plotinus' thinking—the goal is not achieved in what would seem to be the highest thought, the vision of reason, the thinking of the eternal forms or essences. For reason is thought and implies otherness. The One of reason, copy of the undifferentiated One, is both subject and object of thought; its objects are differentiated. Without duality—cleavage and otherness—the One is silence. An immediate self-apprehending of the One would be "a simple, wholly identical act and would bear no relation to thought."

Vision in Plotinus has two meanings: (1) the beholding of the essences in objects, (2) union, beyond thought, with the objectless One. This union is not achieved by thought; in it, thought is transcended and discarded. Thus union with the One is also said to transcend vision.

To rise beyond thinking, beyond reason, beyond Being, to attain to the

One, that is the supreme possibility. It is the center of Plotinus' thinking, and it is from this vantage point that we must seek to understand him. He couches his experience of the One in such statements as the following:

1. "Often when from the slumber of the body I awake to myself and, relinquishing the outer world, hold converse with myself, I behold a marvelous beauty: then more than ever I am assured of community with a higher world, I inwardly enact the noblest life and become one with the godhead. . . . When after that sojourn in the divine, I descend to intellectual activity, I ask myself how it happens that I am now descending and how the soul ever entered into my body, although, even within the body, it is the high thing it has shown itself to be."

2. The union is compared to the experience of the adept who has left the idols behind him and has become one with the divine in the inner sanctuary (*adyton*). There beholding and beheld are one, perfect simplicity, there is no object and no subject. "The beholder has become another, no longer himself and no longer his own." But returned from the *adyton*, he encounters the idols he had left behind him. "Thus these become the second visions."

3. "But there is the truly lovable, with which he who has apprehended it and truly possesses it can remain united, for it is not veiled in flesh and blood. He who has beheld it knows the truth of what I say, namely how the soul receives a new life and needs no other. On the contrary, he must cast off everything else, remain in this alone and become this alone. . . . There we behold God and ourselves, ourselves as pure light, weightless, becoming, or rather being, God."

When, having been one with true being, he returns to this existence, "mindful of his state at the moment of union, he bears within him an image of the One." But when he tries to speak, it will be of a realm outside him, where there was absolute unity without otherness, "and that is why the vision is so hard to describe." The difficulty is "that we cannot gain awareness of the One by means of scientific knowledge or pure thought, but only through a presence which is higher than knowledge." Hence it can be encompassed neither in speech nor in writing. "We speak and write only in order to lead to it, to awaken, to indicate. For instruction serves only to show the way; if you wish to see, you yourself must do the seeing." Plotinus devises increasingly penetrating images for what cannot be adequately expressed.

The beholder was one with the beheld. Thus what took place "was not really a beholding but more in the nature of a union," not with an idol or a likeness, but with God Himself.

Such "beholding" is not thinking, for its subject and object are one. United with the One, I do not think, nor does the One think. This "vision" is greater than reason, before reason, above reason. Here the soul scorns thought, which it otherwise loves so dearly. Satiated with thought, the soul, attaining to the intelligible realm of the *nous,* puts all thoughts behind it.

Nor is this vision life or motion; it is a standing-still, disturbed neither by anger nor by desire. In seclusion the soul is distracted by nothing, nor turned toward itself. "There the soul is not even soul, because the One does not live; it is above life."

Having entered into the perfection of the One, the soul "no longer perceives that it is in a body. Nor does it call itself anything else, not man, nor living creature, nor being, nor the whole."

What is no longer vision, thinking, or life, Plotinus calls a standing-out (*ekstasis*) from oneself, a giving of oneself, a growing-simple (*haplōsis*).

It is a beholding no longer in successive parts, but "all at once." It can "not be perceived with mortal eyes." Filled with God, the soul stands serenely "in solitary repose and without change, nowhere deviating from its essence, not even rotating round itself, everywhere standing fast as though it had become rest itself." "No longer itself nor belonging to itself, it arrives there and belonging to the One it is one with it, communicable to no one apart from those who are themselves favored with vision." It is in such terms that Plotinus speaks of the ineffable.

1. *The impelling force:* Through thought reason (*nous*) perceives what is in it, and by intuition apprehends what is beyond it. Thanks to this intuition, the soul is filled with love and yearning; transcending reason, it becomes drunk in a way that is better than sober earnestness. The soul beholds the One by muddling and dispelling, as it were, its intellective faculty (reason, *nous*). Thus it attains to the One.

2. *Plotinus compares:* In the darkness or through closed eyelids our eye can see a light that has no outside source but springs from within. It sees unseeing, and it is then that it sees most authentically, for it sees light, whereas other things, though light-like, are not light. "Thus reason, in veiling itself from other things and withdrawing within itself, will see unseeing; it will not see another light in something other, but a pure light of its own, which suddenly flares up from within."

3. *Place and time disappear:* When reason sees without seeing, when the One is suddenly manifested, reason does not know where it comes from, whether from without or within. And when the vision has passed, reason says: It was within and yet not within. We must not ask whence. For there is no Whence. For it does not come and does not go; rather, it appears at one moment, and at another it does not appear. It came like one who does not come, for it was not seen as we see one who has come but as we see one who has always been present. We must not try to pursue it, but quietly, preparing ourselves for the vision, wait for it to appear as the eye awaits the sunrise. Without coming it is miraculously here and nowhere; yet where it is not, there is nothing! The soul in this life shuts itself off; not so the One.—Only from its memory of the timeless Being in which it

forever partakes does the soul know of the One, in moments when time is extinguished—such moments are not units of time. Here the soul finds no "place," but spaceless presence. "He (God, the One) raises them so high that they are neither in a place nor anywhere where one thing is in another." The One is nowhere. "For what is not somewhere is nowhere absent. . . . If it is not absent from any thing and yet is not somewhere, it must be everywhere, self-subsisting. It is whole and it is everywhere; no thing has it and yet every thing has it, that is to say, *it* has every thing."

In all our thinking we involuntarily employ spatial images that are often misleading. As Plotinus explicitly states, we posit a space and introduce the One into it. Then we ask how it got there, assuming that it must have come from above or below. But our vision of the One must be spaceless; we must not situate it in any space whatever, whether eternally at rest within it or recently arrived there; rather, we must presume that space, like all other determinations, comes afterward. In thus thinking the spaceless One, we do not surround it with something. In our representations, to be sure, everything takes on a spatial character and has its place, but in reality space belongs only to the last stage of knowledge, the stage of nature.

4. "*In the One there is no deception.* What can the soul find that is truer than the true? It is what it says, and it says this later; it says it silently, and it is not deceived in its well-being. Nor does it say this because the body feels well-being, but because it has become what it was when it was happy."

What Plotinus calls perfection, the source and goal, is for him absolute reality, the highest stage, not Being, but before all Being. The soul knows its authentic Being. It knows that its customary state of consciousness is a decline. But in its participation in the source, it experiences deep satisfaction: transcending everything that is, it experiences what has no further goal beyond it. Plotinus' writings are an unexcelled record of this fundamental experience, which is understood and produced by philosophical thinking. The experience he pursues is not one that is enjoyed as an event in time; it pervades all the moments of existence and is the source of all meaning; it is the absolute consciousness which imprints finite consciousness. He actually experienced as a perfect whole what in this immanent world we can know only in the duality of loving and loved, beholding and beheld, that is, he experienced the goal that gives our imperfect yearning its direction.

This experience seems to permit of psychological description, but it is essentially different from any describable psychological experience. It is not a drunken clouding of consciousness nor a passing sensual euphoria. It is a vision which presupposes intellectual activity, but is realized only when we transcend reason, not when we sink beneath it. In my most lucid, superlucid consciousness my certainty of belonging to a higher world ceases to be a mere belief; this world becomes actually present. Such lucidity is not a state akin to sleeping or dreaming, from which I awaken to everyday consciousness, which I take as the norm in attempting to interpret a puzzling state. The reverse is true. This state is experienced rather as a waking from the customary mists of existence into another existence, in which I rise above my usual thinking, spatiotemporal experience.

Yet we are told that this state sets in at particular moments. This seems paradoxical, for how can an experience which transcends all experience and is by definition beyond time take place in time? It is Porphyry, to be sure, who speaks of four definite instances. Plotinus himself tells us only that he had the experience "often." What, according to Porphyry, would seem to have been a rare, anomalous experience is, in the statement of Plotinus, the natural reality, which gives all existence its meaning.

Though for Plotinus himself this experience transcends all experience, it inevitably raises a psychological question once it is localized in time. We inquire into its nature and possible causes and look for parallels. But in Plotinus we find no trace of abnormal psychic states, no description of abnormal sensations or visions, of involuntary seizure by an overpowering force, no word of any symptoms that may have struck the attention of those around him. He speaks of no artificial measures, no physical devices or techniques of meditation, employed to induce states of ecstasy.

Ecstatic states and mystical experiences play an important part in the history of all cultures. They are a field of psychological observation in which certain basic forms of experience always recur. Plotinus' transcending of thought seems to differ from such experience. His accounts contain the barest minimum of psychological phenomena and no psychopathological indications whatever. One is impressed by the simplicity of his communication from the depths. What Plotinus describes is the summit of his whole thinking. It is not an isolated, anomalous state, but the completion and confirmation of his intellectual life. Even without any special experience, localized in time, it would still be an effective picture of the ultimate perfection which is always present in transcending love and vision, as disclosed in temporary psychological processes.

But if, as is possible, Plotinus' experience can be explained in psychological terms, the question arises whether in Plotinus such experience, which is also to be met with elsewhere, derives from his philosophizing a meaning it would otherwise not have. For psychological states, whether universal or abnormal, may either be ignored as irrelevant or may, by being interpreted in connection with a man's life, take on extraordinary significance. Thus, after certain states are observed by psychological methods, the question of interpretation remains, and this cannot be answered by psychological observation and experience. The question of meaning cannot be decided by the methods of psychology. Seemingly identical psychological states may conceal very different extra-psychological impulses—one may prove to be an utterly meaningless experience, while the other may be the beginning of a profound, lifelong certainty. In Plotinus the realities of love and vision, transcending the world and yet enacted in the world, derive their meaning from his interpretation of his ecstatic experience. This interpretation is enacted in the realm of the Supreme One, which, whether directly experienced or merely constructed, derives its meaning from, and lends new meaning to, existential experience in the world.

The stages of knowledge are actualized in experience. They range from lowest to highest, from unseeing perception of darkness to' union with the One. Are we then dealing with a subjective hierarchy extending from sensory perception to *unio mystica* rather than with degrees of being, from nonbeing to Above-Being? For Plotinus there is no such alternative of subjective and objective. At every level like is recognized by like, and every level is a human potentiality. Thus the scale of Being, from matter (nonbeing) to the One (Above-Being), is actualized in the stages of man's knowledge.

Ecstasy as a state of consciousness corresponds to the One, a thought construction situated beyond all thinkables. The stages of Being have their correlates in the lower levels of knowledge; they stand in the same relation to ecstasy as do the levels of being to Above-Being. As in conceptual thinking the One is not cogitated in itself but only in its derivatives; as in the temple cult the formless godhead of the *adyton* is manifested only indirectly through the divine images, so it is only through love and vision, as enacted in the world, that the ecstasy of *henōsis* (*unio*) becomes accessible to retrospective and prospective self-awareness.

V. SPECULATIVE TRANSCENDING

To philosophize is to think. The thinkable is an intermediate realm at whose limits the unthinkable is encountered. If this limit is surpassed in moments of union with the One, such moments are arrived at by thought, and, as long as man is engaged in temporal existence, they are followed by a return to thought.

For Plotinus thought has no other purpose than such union with the One. Consequently he seeks knowledge of the things of this world, not for their own sake, but only in order to transcend them. But this itself requires a wide range of thought in the world. A philosopher should "not reduce the divine to a point. God has revealed Himself in breadth and fullness." Man cannot abide in the One. Accordingly, all recorded philosophy consists in exercises of thought, schematic images, and constructions of total Being. All these serve as guides by which to arrive at the One and, on returning, means by which to retain the presence of the one and only essential.

In Plotinus we find three main elements, whose consequences are intertwined in his metaphysical thinking: (1) a system of categories peculiar to him (the preparation); (2) methods of categorial transcending (the principles of a thinking that shatters against the unthinkable); (3) a thinking in images of the All (rest in objective contemplation).

1. The categories: What I think and have before me as an object "is." The self-evident appears to me as "Being." But what "is" Being? With this question I turn away from objective, self-evident thinking to examine the meaning of Being in all that is thought and thinkable. I set out to elucidate Being, without new objective knowledge. Plotinus supports Aristotle's thesis "that Being is not synonymous in all things." The categories serve to distinguish and classify the different kinds of Being. The purpose of each category is to characterize a mode or class of Being, for example, substantive Being, qualitative Being, quantitative Being, etc. The statement that something is (or the term Being) does not always mean the same thing. But is there a total body of categories which develop coherently from a principle and can be conceived as parts or classes of the one Being?

What may be called Plotinus' doctrines of categories is on the surface an aggregate. He found doctrines of categories originating in Plato, elaborated by Aristotle, modified by the Stoics. In his system, he stresses only one original point. He puts forward a radical critique of all his predecessors (with the exception of Plato): "In their classification they do not speak of the intelligible; thus they did not attempt to classify all modes of Being, but disregarded the most important." For Plotinus there are only two classes of thinkable Being: the sensory and the intelligible. Intelligible Being is Being par excellence, archetypal Being; sensory Being is only reflected and secondary. In considering every category, we must ask to which class of Being it applies, the sensory or the intelligible, or to both, whether it is rooted in one and transferable to the other, or whether it is specific to the one and not transferable.

In Plotinus only these two levels of Being are subject to the categories. They are encompassed by nonbeing and Above-Being, which cannot be grasped in categories. Nor has the soul any category of its own, it occupies a middle position in which everything, from Above-Being to nonbeing, comes together in a totality. But of course Plotinus requires categories when it comes to thinking this middle position and describing the soul. The question arises: Do other categories than those occurring in the sensory and intelligible world crop up in the process?

Plotinus' doctrine of categories is a composite of Plato and Aristotle. To the intelligible world pertain the five categories of Plato's *Sophist:* Being, identity and difference, motion and rest; to the sensory world apply the ten Aristotelian categories (in particular, substance, quantity, place and time, action and passivity, relation).

The division of the categories into those of the sensory and the supersensory world cuts across another classification: on the one hand the categories that reside in the thing itself (motion, rest, quality, quantity, etc.), on the other hand, the subjective categories (the *katēgorēmata*), namely, the categories of relation.

The two categorial worlds are not parallel. The categories of the sensory world disappear in the intelligible world and are not transferable to it. Those of the intelligible world, however, are present in the sensory world, but not in the same way—the difference is that between archetype and copy.

In the intelligible world the fundamental categories are identity and difference. They occur also in the sensory world, but here they signify estrangement, the separation of the many things from one another, while in the intelligible world the opposites are not only logically connected, they are one.

This transformation of one and the same category from intelligible archetype to copy, that takes place in the sensory world, is brought about by space, time, and matter. Free from space and time, the intelligible categories subsist in the unity of opposites. Here, consequently, there is no separation among things; they are not isolated from one another and do not clash with one another. With space comes separation, with time generation and transience. In the sensory world, matter is the principle of formlessness which disrupts the formed figures, and of separation which dissolves their unity. The things of the sensory world are not only thought but must also be perceived. Thought and being are no longer identical.

2. Categorial transcending: This doctrine of categories is itself a means of transcending from the sensory to the intelligible. But this transcending, still within the realm of the thinkable, is only the first step in his doctrine of categories.

The next and final step consists in a transcending to the unthinkable, a thinking of the unthinkable. This is possible only if the thinker's orientation in the thinkable is such that the thinkable becomes a jumping-off place. The thinkable can be transcended only with the help of elucidated thinkables. In this transcending the thinkable world must shatter, but this does not mean that thought gives way to a confused stammering; the thinkable is surpassed by the methods of dialectical speculation.

Thus Plotinus does not content himself with the orientation in the thinkable world provided by his system of categories. He makes use of other categories, borrowed from traditional philosophy, which are not explicitly included in his doctrine. These are: form and matter, reality and potentiality, cause, life, and others. Plotinus has given us an abundance of speculations in this direction. A few examples:

Unity: Everything that exists in the world is a unity of many. The amazing principle that makes a thing one must be fundamental. "All beings are beings by virtue of unity. What could exist at all except as one? Neither an army, nor a chorus, nor a flock can be without unity, nor is there any house or ship without it. The same is true of plants and animals, each of which forms a unity." Without unity all these—army, chorus, flock, house, ship, plant, animal—cease to be. "Health, too, is the condition of a body acting as a co-ordinate unity. Beauty appears when limbs and features are controlled by this principle, unity; moral excellence is present when a soul acts as a concordant total, brought to unity."

His wonderment at this universal unity, through which each being—in itself a multiplicity—becomes a thing, the mystery of this "one out of many," leads Plotinus to the transcending leap: each particular unity comes about through an absolute One, a principle of unity. It is through the transcendent One that every existing thing is one.

No unity in the world of existence is the One. Rather, each thing or being derives its rank in the scale of reality from its particular mode of being-one. "Among the things that are said to be one, each is one in a particular way, according to its nature." Thus the unity of the soul varies with its rank and authenticity, but even the highest, most authentic soul is different from the One and is not the One itself. Similarly, things are nearer to the One or farther away from it according to the manner of their unity. "The discrete, a flock, for example, is farther from the One, the continuous is closer to it; the soul is in still closer bond with it." Things partake of the One, they are not the One itself. "When we apprehend the unity of plants, i.e. the enduring principle, and the unity of animals and the unity of the soul, and the unity of the all, in each case we are apprehending what is strongest and most valuable in those things."

Transcending all modes of unity in the thinkable world, Plotinus arrives at the one itself (*hen*) and questions it. At this point begins his speculative dialectic: What one thinks in the category of unity ought to be transcendence itself. But once thought, once conceived as a category, the One always takes on a finite meaning: The One is opposed to the other; the number one is opposed to the numerical series; the one that makes many into one is opposed to the many. In any of these finite meanings, the One is no longer the transcendent One. In each case it ceases to be the absolute One, for it is always at the same time not-one, because it is connected with the other, with the numerical series, the multiplicity of the manifold. Consequently Plotinus discards every finite meaning of the One, which he retains only as a name (*hen*) for something which defies all thinking in finite meanings.

The absolute One is necessarily beyond the One and the Other, beyond numbers, beyond multiplicity; this Unity is the source of all modes of unity, including the oneness of the number One. But even to speak of the source leads to a finite categorial manifestation of the One, which, though useful as a means of expression, must be surpassed at every step.

This form of transcending thought, which negates all finite contents, is frequently met with on the summits of speculation. Kant conceives of the unity of transcendental synthesis as the principle of all categorial formation, but goes on to say that this unity is not the category of unity; it is what makes the category of "unity" possible. Similarly Plotinus calls upon us to think by means of a category (unity) what is not itself within the category. In the mere name of the One the category is left behind, but perhaps the name thereby takes on a richer meaning. Plotinus transcends from the category of identity (*tautotēs,* which can also be translated as unity) and difference (*heterotēs*) to the unity that is the ground of both. Schelling will speak of the unity of unity and opposition, Hegel of the identity of identity and nonidentity (difference). The unthinkable is circled around with formulations: the One and the Other are not each for itself, rather, the One is with itself in the Other; clarifying one another, they are a totality; thinking and what is thought, subject and object, are not differentiated. Here we have a rich and complex world of logical thinking, which always derives its meaning from its one goal: to shatter against unthinkableness, which alone touches upon the essential.

Form and matter: Thanks to the artist, the shapeless marble takes on form as a statue. By analogy, all perceptible being is considered as a whole, consisting of intelligible form and the matter to which it gives shape. In every object of thought, even in mathematical figures and numbers, a distinction is made between form and matter. The opposition proves to be universal. In every existing or thinkable thing the two factors are present, but in an ascending scale, so that what in one case is form becomes matter in relation to another form (marble is in itself formed matter, but becomes matter in relation to the form of the artist). Using this pair of categories, form and matter, Plotinus transcends in two steps:

a) *From the sensory to the intelligible:* All existents are form and matter. "The lowest part of every thing is its matter, for which reason it is utterly dark." But the existent is either intelligible, eternal, free from time and space, or else it is sensuous, coming into being and passing away in time and space. Hence there are two matters. The darkness of the intelligible world differs from that of the spatiotemporal, sensory world. "The matter pertaining to the two worlds is different, and likewise the form." For the divine matter that receives the definition of form has itself a definite, thinking life. Earthly matter receives definition, but it does not take on life and thought, it is formed but dead. In the intelligible world matter is wholly formed, in the sensory world a part of it is recalcitrant to form. Intelligible matter lends itself only to the higher principle; sensuous matter contains an element of resistance. In the intelligible world matter is everything at once, there is no form it cannot take, for it has everything in itself. Sensuous matter is everything possible by turns, but in each case it is only a particular thing. Intelligible matter is eternally the same, sensuous matter takes on ever new forms.

The essential difference between archetypal, intelligible matter and ectypal, sensuous matter is this: "There above, quasi-matter is also form, just as the soul, too, is form, yet in relation to something other it is matter."

In the intelligible world form and matter are equally eternal. They are both created in so far as they have a source, increate in so far as their source is not situated in time.

b) *Beyond form and matter:* By way of form Plotinus arrives at what is no longer form, because it is without matter, the Supreme One. By way of matter he arrives at what is no longer matter, because it is without form, the nonbeing of matter. Plotinus transcends the form-matter relationship by dissolving it.

These two processes of transcending have one thing in common. In both thought takes a step that is an end of thought. In both the unthinkable is ineffable, formless. "What is this nonexisting thing? We must depart from it in silence and, leaving our opinion uncertain, cease to inquire further." This statement applies to both directions of transcending.

When I think, I think in terms of form and matter. In transcending I strive to think pure form and the mere matter of nonthinking. What is thought in this way is outside of all being. But at the opposite poles, Above-Being and nonbeing are named.

But since all existents are rooted in something that is not an existent, the nonexistent cannot in either case be nothing. The nonbeing of matter is not nothing (not an *ouk on* but a *mē on*). Plotinus writes: "But the nonexistent is not absolute nonbeing, but only something other than Being; it is as nonexistent as a copy of Being, or far more nonexistent." So much for matter. Above-Being, the One, is also called nonbeing (*mē on*). The "above" indicates the direction of transcending; in content it too is a negation of being: "This miracle confronting the mind is the One, because it *is* nonbeing (*mē on*)." The same operation of thought leads to opposite extremes.

Where thought is transcended, the One is apprehended by more-than-thinking, in fulfillment by *ekstasis, haplōsis, henōsis.* Contact with matter, on the other hand, is achieved neither by sensory perception nor by thinking, but by a less-than-thinking, an "inauthentic thinking" (Plato), as when the eye sees darkness.

The essential difference lies in what I myself am in the two opposite processes of transcending. In confronting matter, I think unthinking; with the undefined within me, I think the undefined outside me; I am lost. When I confront the One, the failure of my thinking raises me above all thinking.

For Plotinus true transcendence is disclosed only in the One and in the soaring of the spirit, and not in the other direction, which is characterized only as nonbeing, deficiency, privation. The parallel between the formal operations leading to failure in both directions might admit of the notion that, concealed in this outward polarity, the one transcendence occurs in both directions. But there is no explicit statement of this notion in Plotinus.

Potentiality and actuality: Logical impossibility (the contradictory) is distinguished from what is really impossible (for lack of foundation in reality) and a corresponding distinction is made between logical and real potentiality. What is logically possible may not be really possible. Real potentiality is considered as passive matter, capable of receiving form, or as inactive energy or latent capacity; these real possibilities are themselves reality, but they are not fulfilled reality.

We seem to be transcending when we conceive the totality of being as the totality of potentialities, from which actuality springs. Here it is assumed that all actuality is possible, but that every potentiality is not actual. Plotinus follows this line of reasoning in a first step: "The Supreme was beyond Being. It is only the potentiality (*dynamis*) of all things; their actuality begins with the Second (Spirit)."

But Plotinus' speculative transcending culminates in a radically different answer to the question concerning the First: The One is self-sufficient, perfect, undivided. "For no one will say that there is a potential One and an actual One. It would be absurd, in the realm of essential reality, to posit different classes of nature by distinguishing between potentiality and actuality." In other words: at their source, beyond all existents, potentiality and actuality are one. A logical relation (potentiality and actuality) serves as a metaphor for something unfathomable. In seeking to express an intuition of the unfathomable in terms of a thought content, we must avoid the distinction between potentiality and actuality that is indispensable in our thinking of existents. Thus we arrive at the logically absurd proposition (for which Cusanus coined the word *"possest"*) that potentiality and actuality are identical.

It is only from our own standpoint, as from existence in the world we look upon the source, that we see the source as the anterior potentiality, followed by the actual existence of the world. As though it were possible to occupy an outside vantage point, from which to survey the source and the process of the world's unfolding, we even go so far as to suppose that our world achieved actuality by virtue of a choice from among the totality of potentialities present in the source. Plotinus does not go to such lengths, though he does allow himself to consider the process from our point of view. "While the Supreme subsists in its own nature, a second energy takes on independent existence." What is true of all existents—"A part of the energy of each thing is contained in its Being and a part moves outward from its Being"—applies equally to the emergence of the spirit and hence of all existents from the One. But whatever Plotinus thinks in this connection is overshadowed by the true transcending in which thought shatters against the identity of potentiality and actuality.

The ground: Every thought content is subject to the questions: Why? Whereby? Whence? To what end? "Ground" is the category of the answers to such questions.

In response to the question: What is the ground of all Being? Plotinus answers: That which is beyond Being. And if asked: Whence this Beyond-

Being?—he replies: In the source, Being and the ground of Being are one. Further questioning is futile. In other words: The category of the "ground" becomes a form of transcending by virtue of the idea: "ground of itself."

For the understanding this idea is a contradiction or a vicious circle. For a ground is no longer a ground when it is said to be identical with what it grounds. By eliminating the questions "whence" and "why," this idea in transcending encounters the ungrounded Being which, precisely because it is ungrounded, ceases to be Being and becomes the ground of Being. This ground of Being cannot be thought as a knowable thing. For then the understanding, which questions each thing as to its ground, would be right. Since the understanding looks upon everything that exists for it, that is, every thinkable, as an object, it must refuse to eliminate the why and the whence. Either it must deny the object—and rightly so when asked to objectify the unthinkable—or it must inquire further as to its ground. Whatever object is set before it or created by it, the understanding cannot stop questioning.

The idea of the unthinkable is possible only through the failure of the understanding. This statement is itself a tautology. Its meaning is not apprehended by the understanding, but through the failure of the understanding, by reason. For the understanding it is nothing; it is fulfilled from out of another source. The transcending idea, an impossibility from the standpoint of the understanding, posits two entities, being and the ground of being, and goes on to say that they are not two but one. By way of clarifying this idea, Plotinus circles around it with the help of other categories—contingency, necessity, freedom, selfness.

"What has its ground in itself" is not contingent—precisely because it has its ground in itself. Nor may we say that it is necessary, for it is free, because it owes its Being to itself. But then again it does not possess freedom, because it is the ground of freedom, not free but something more than freedom. It is situated beyond those modes of being which we, in connection with existent things, regard as contingent, necessary, or free. It is itself. Plotinus has impressive formulations of all these ideas.

Contingency: Concerning the "One," the "First," we are not justified in saying: "That is how it happened." The First cannot be contingent, for contingency "prevails in the derived and the many." Contingency "comes from the Other and first makes its appearance in the world of becoming."

The First, which has nothing outside it or before it, might be called contingent if measured by a preceding, thinkable necessity, such as a natural law or a rational plan. But such a law or plan does not precede the First but follows from it.

To speak of the contingency of the First can be meaningful only if the category of "contingency" is disrupted. The "contingency" of the First would not be an accident obstructing the above-mentioned laws, but would be something preceding and conditioning them. What logical thought, which transforms everything into the thinkable, regards as contingent because it cannot be derived, would then become meaningful, the source of necessity as well as freedom; it would be the contingency of all natural laws and laws of freedom.

Contingency is the category of what cannot be understood on the basis of any necessity or rationality. But in the world contingency is an expression of failure to understand for want of the knowledge that is indispensable in the finite world. In transcendence it becomes a symbol for the fullest meaning of the incomprehensible.

Necessity: But if we now conceive of the One as necessity, in contradistinction to contingency, the proposition will be: It is not by chance no other than what it is; it is what it is by necessity. But by this definition, it would again lose what makes it the First.

It did not have to be, because it was the source of everything that had to be. It did not have to be; rather, everything else, including necessity, had to wait for it.

It would be wrong to say that the First is not master of its own becoming, if only "because it never became." But in no respect may we say that "this first nature is not master of what it is; that it does not take what it is from itself; that it does or does not do what it is compelled to do or not to do." For it "is not restrained by necessity; rather, it is itself necessity and for other things the law." But it would also be wrong to conclude that this necessity brought itself into existence: it does not even exist, for all existence came into existence after the First and for the sake of the First. The First is what it is, not because it cannot be different, but because it is the best. Plotinus finally arrives at the following formula: "The Good created itself. For if the will sprang from the Good and is its work, the Good provided its own hypostasis. Consequently it is what itself willed." Is the First then freedom?

Freedom: Freedom would then seem to be the category appropriate to the First. But the category of freedom has something incomprehensible about it, which sets it apart from all those categories which make objects of knowledge possible. Thus it is the principle of an entirely different group of categories. That is why in reference to the First Plotinus speaks very differently of freedom than of the other categories, but also why he ultimately withdraws this category along with the others, so resolutely safeguarding the unthinkable ground of all things against all determination.

The first step: Rising up from our own freedom, we think the perfect freedom of the First: We know ourselves to be free, but divided. We are composite, not an original substance (*ousia*), "hence we are not masters of our own substance . . . substance is one thing, we are another . . . substance governs us. . . . But since in a way we ourselves are this substance that governs us, we may be called masters of ourselves." From our freedom we take the step to the freedom of the One. "That which is wholly what it is, at one with its substance, is governed by its own Being and no longer contingent on something else." Undivided, it is perfectly free. The One "is inconceivable otherwise than willing to be what it is. It coincides with itself, for it wills to be itself and is what it wills."

In the second step, the transcending continues, but the positive statements about the freedom of the One are withdrawn. No more than any other predicate is the predicate "free" applicable to the One. Like all other formulable concepts—the beautiful, the venerable, thinking, or Being—free will and freedom are also posterior to the One. For freedom implies effect on something else, it implies that something else exists, and that the effect, if free, is unobstructed. But the One must be posited outside all relation.

These two steps are repeated: Our consciousness of freedom resides in our striving toward the Good. If freedom is striving toward the Good, we cannot deny freedom to that which is itself the supreme Good. It would be still more absurd to deny freedom to the Good itself, the One, on the ground that it remains within itself, feeling no need to move toward something other. But if we say that the freedom of the One is directed toward itself, what we know as our freedom vanishes. We choose ourselves on the basis of models and standards. But the One cannot be thought of in this way. "Even if we assume that it chooses what it wishes to become, that it is free to transform its own nature into something other, we are not entitled to suppose that it would wish to become something other." For "Where there is no two-as-one, but only One—there can be no self-mastery." "The Good is the willing of itself; it chooses itself, because no other is present to exert a necessary attraction upon it."

Our choosing and willing of ourselves must have its ground in the First, but it is not in the First. The First is "the truly self-governing power which is what it wills," or rather, as Plotinus makes haste to add, "which relegates its will to the world of existence, whereas in itself it is greater than all willing and leaves willing behind it."

Itself: The One which "in a manner of speaking creates itself, rests on itself, and looks upon itself," "has nothing other, but is itself alone." "Other things are in themselves inadequate to being, but even in its isolation this (the One) is what it is." Just as it is above reason, it is above freedom and independence. What for us finite rational beings is a formula for evil (*Richard III:* "I am I") becomes in transcending thought the supernal principle which is the source of personal, loving, free life; yet it is not this life itself, but more than this life, its ground. "Thus everything came forth from a source which did not reflect but all at once provided the ground and with it being." This First "is itself the ground of itself, through itself and for its own sake; for it is originally itself and superessentially itself." "Itself": that is the last word.

The formulas for this being which is alone and entirely itself, but lacks all determination, hence every predicate, are tautologies: "It is what it is" (as Yahweh says: "I am that I am"), that is, it has no determination, because all determination applies to something particular, ensuing, posterior. "Concerning what thus has not issued from itself, but everlastingly belongs to itself, we may say in the most eminent sense: it is what it is." It is unique in its kind, but not because there are other kinds beside it, "but because it is itself and well pleased as it were with itself, and has nothing better than itself."

In human existence such transcending thought kindles that spark of the self which in all flux and dispersion knows itself to be itself through identification with a Being that is beyond all Being, untouched by all the comings and goings of existence, not even subject to the timeless intelligible categories, but the ground of these too. Like is recognized by like. Accordingly: "If each thing makes itself into something, it becomes clear that that [the One] is primarily and originally a principle whereby all other things can be through themselves."

All questioning into the ground of the One takes place in the shattering category of the ground that is groundless. "It did not come in order that you should ask: How did it come? What fate brought it about? For before it there was neither fate nor chance."

Life: Plotinus sees life in plants, animals, man. Happiness is the lot of those who live in higher degree: In the world of existence, the best is the authentic and perfect life. The question of what this life is points to the supersensory source. Though experienced and seen in this world, life has its source in the intelligible. If I wish to understand life, I must transcend toward the intelligible: the perfect, authentic, and real life resides in intelligible nature; all other life is imperfect, a mere reflection of life, incomplete, impure. This perfect life is the life of the *nous,* it is itself thought. In the descending scale of life as well as of thoughts, the degree of darkness increases. But the "bright and first life and the first spirit are one. A first thought then is the first life, and the second life is a second thought, and the last life is a last thought."

But in transcending toward the original life, the philosophical eye sees how "vital energy extends everywhere and is nowhere absent." Existence is permeated by life, it is not dead, but life diminishes by degrees in a scale descending to the dead. Dead is what cannot create something else, as for example the last concept, and above all matter: even when informed, it does not "become a living, thinking thing, but a kind of decorated corpse."

Because the true life is the first life, the immaterial life of the soul in the *nous,* it does not die. But life belongs to the existent, i.e., to the intermediate realm between Above-Being and nonbeing. Hence life goes beyond itself, but in two opposite directions: toward More-than-life in the One of

Above-Being and toward death in the nonbeing of matter. Hence the ambiguity of death, which ambiguity is annulled in transcending: for death is more and less than life, the fullness of Above-Being and the emptiness of nonbeing. Life rises to fulfillment in the transcendent source of life and in death becomes nothingness.

It would be interesting to develop this speculative transcending into a comprehensive system. Instead, we shall have to limit ourselves to a few aspects that may clarify the examples cited above.

Plotinus' classification of the categories into those of the sensory and those of the intelligible world allows him to feel at home in the intelligible cosmos of eternal forms. We do not conceive this cosmos of Ideas as something strange and alien; rather, it is present in our thinking of the intelligible. The intelligible cosmos is not an object for us; rather, our thinking participates in it. If Being is present in thinking and pure thought strikes at the heart of Being, logical structure becomes the structure of Being. Thinking in the categories apprehends the essence of Being.

But all this takes place in the vestibule. The true transcending, the part of Plotinus' thinking that is not (like the differentiation of the two categorial worlds) a didactic exercise but a fundamental operation of thought, is something radically different, namely the striving to go beyond both groups of categories, beyond the sensory world and the cosmos of the intelligible to Above-Being and nonbeing.

The methods employed in practice, though Plotinus never sets them forth with full systematic awareness, are as follows:

Certain categories are involuntarily absolutized (unity, the ground, potentiality, life, etc.) and so for a moment take on a depth that surpasses their actual meaning, as though they were possessed of real existence. The transformation of a category into the ultimate ground of all things annuls its determinateness and qualitative particularity. But since, objectively considered, the category remains a determinate category, since as such it is only a false absolute, thinking in this category takes on a form in which every statement is destroyed by an inner contradiction, or else antagonistic categories are posited as identical. The rigid categories of the spiritual cosmos take on a fluidity (or surpass and destroy themselves) by becoming the basis of transcending operations leading to the One.

Whatever category is employed in the thinking of transcendence, it is inapplicable as a determinate category, while in becoming indeterminate it ceases to be thinkable. "Even if we were to say, it is the Good and the simplest, we shall, though speaking the truth, be making no clear statement, as long as we have no point of support for our thinking." But in respect of our thinking, such a "point of support" is at once the condition of its objective clarity and the germ of its speculative untruth.

What is said is taken back. To every sentence, Plotinus tells us, an "as it were" must be added. "For purposes of persuasion," names are used, "and in our expression we are entitled to deviate somewhat from rigorous thinking." On pain of remaining silent, there is no other possibility for discourse: "It is thus that we must speak of God, since we cannot speak of him as we should like to."

As we follow these contradictory thoughts that ultimately dissolve into nothing, we may be tempted to suppose that, because they have no object, they are only empty and meaningless discourse. In answer to this, it must be said that these are methods whose meaning lies in a fulfillment that transcends thought.

A mind conscious of transcendence can achieve clarity through operations of thought, without objective knowledge—for transcendence cannot be known as an object. On the dividing line between world and transcendence, the thinker surpasses his consciousness of this limit: with logical methods which may be purely formal from the standpoint of the mere understanding, he enriches his awareness of the superabundance, depth, inexplicability of transcendence, while at every step the nonabsoluteness of all thinkables without exception becomes more compellingly evident. An obscure, formal consciousness of the limit is transformed into a radiant, real, and effective consciousness.

In the objective world, I continually think Being. This is never the ultimate Being. And so I go further. In the ascent from one to the other, from every attainment to its ground, my understanding can find no beginning and source. I should have to decide on an ultimate, and at this arbitrarily chosen point cease to question. Only if, instead of rising *ad infinitum* in this series from object to object, I effect a leap by transcending from object to nonobject, can I, without fixating an object, meditate my way into the source, dreaming as I think. This is what Plotinus does: his First is not an object, it is without predicate and cannot be thought. It is not the first member of a series. To think it is not to think it. Thus in the pursuit of each category it becomes necessary to effect a leap into the realm where thinking ceases. The thinking of the understanding leads to the endless. But transcending thought arrives at the source or goal where it finds rest.

The dialectic of this thinking that aspires to become nonthinking results in: a shift of thinking into inability to think; a thinking that negates itself and so transcends itself as thinking; a nonthinking which in ceasing to think something, does not think nothing, but thinks the nonbeing that is not Being or Above-Being. This dialectic that continually transcends itself is a specific kind of thinking, meaningless as long as objectivity and intuition are the conditions of meaning, but essential for the elucidation of the consciousness of Being and its limit.

This speculative dialectic achieves a meaningful failure in the failure of discourse. Meaningful, first because it makes us receptive to that which cannot be apprehended as a thinkable, and second, because it enables us to think the thinkables in such a way as to free ourselves from them and overcome our tendency to find an ultimate and absolute in any object of thought.

All speculative thinking as a logical construction has been and always will be doomed to failure, if what is expected is a knowledge of something, a derivation, an understanding of one thing through another, a determination in categories. However, such thinking derives new meaning from the consequence of its failure. Yet this meaning cannot be preserved in dogmas, but only through participation in the thinking of the creative metaphysicians, which is always unique, though it loses its radiance and power in being expounded and analyzed. Still, exposition and analysis are indispensable, for they alone can provide us with the equipment with which to understand the wonderful language of the great metaphysicians.

3. Transcending in images of the All: The movement of transcending achieves rest and contemplation in almost tangible images of the One, of Spirit, and Nature. The movements that have led to this point are forgotten. The levels of being are disclosed not through the process of search, but through vision. At this point there is no cleavage between mythical vision and logical clarity. Just as the image becomes a metaphor for what cannot be stated in terms of rational thought, so thought itself becomes a logical myth. These schemas of Plotinus' poetic truth accept philosophical responsibility for their truthfulness and are illumined, in their form and method, by this philosophical earnestness. To put the main emphasis on the logical myth (as in our initial representation of the Plotinian system) would be to neglect the other, more essential pole of this thinking: the sublime forms of speculative transcending, the ascent of the soul by way of thought.

The traditional myths and mysteries were not indifferent to Plotinus. As in Plato, the yoke of mythology is thrown off, transformed into a sovereign capacity for thinking in myths, which enables him to make traditional myths his own. This use of mythology plays a minor role in Plotinus, but it does occur (and was developed into a deceptive and increasingly empty system by the Neoplatonists).

VI. FALL AND RESURGENCE

Philosophy is vision and speculative dialectic, and in both cases a purification of the soul. The aim of philosophy is not merely to know Being and the world, but through this knowledge to lift up the soul. The soul has the alternative of slipping downward or of rising upward.

In present existence the soul is moved by a drive to transcend all things and attain to the realm where there is perfect union. Filled with loathing for the fetters that bind us to this existence, it yearns to hasten away. When the soul is seized with intense love of that place, it "casts off every form it has, even the intelligible form." Only when the soul has freed itself from what it has, is the One suddenly revealed to it.

But no will can induce immediate union with the One by design. It comes as a gift. To seize it directly is "to fly as in a dream." In so doing, I merely close myself off from the possibility of becoming God. The human soul can become God "only insofar as the Spirit leads it upward; any attempt to go beyond the Spirit involves a fall into the spiritless."

Here, in this existence, accordingly, we must content ourselves with little. The only possibility of philosophizing lies in contemplation of the One in the spiritual archetypes and beyond these in the speculative dialectic of self-negating thoughts. We are limited to the upward path of the knowing soul in the world. If I aspire to see the One, I must look upon "the divine images closer to the periphery." Before the First, the One, I must stop short of the First, the One, "and say nothing more concerning it, but inquire how things came into being after it." The greatness of the One is to be seen in that "which is after it and for its sake."

Anyone who has been in the realm of perfection, says Plotinus, knows whither his yearning tends. There the flame was kindled, which dies down when man redescends. "Why does man not remain there? Because he has not wholly departed from here," because he is still "weighed down by the body's unrest."

But if in this existence he has achieved an encounter with the One, a tension arises between his yearning and his resignation. The fundamental attitude of the soul is transformed. It has knowledge of the essential. When it is there and has itself become the object of its yearning, "there is nothing for which it would exchange this gift, even if someone were to offer it the whole of heaven, for there is nothing better. . . . For the soul can rise no higher, and only in its descent can it see those other things." From that realm, a shadow of vanity falls upon all things in this world. "When the soul is united with it (the One) and ceases to behold anything at all, it fears no misfortune. Even if everything round it should perish, this would only mean the fulfilment of its desire to be alone with the One." Recollection of the One changes the whole world. "Everything else in which the soul formerly took pleasure, glory, power, wealth, beauty, science: upon all this it looks with contempt and says as much."

Plotinus' metaphysics is at once speculative knowledge and elevation of the soul. His knowledge of transcendence is inseparable from his consciousness of his own freedom. The soul is not in a final state. It is fallen. It can fall still lower, or it can return.

If, in considering Plotinus' vision, we start from his cosmic schema, we find all being engaged in an eternal and necessary cycle of descent and ascent, from the Above-Being of the One to the Nonbeing of matter and back again. In this system freedom seems to be a foreign element. The cosmic vision does not explain why individual souls, endowed with wills of their own, break loose from the All-Soul, why, in addition to the necessary descent of the cycle, there is a falling of the individual soul.

But conversely, if we take Plotinus' consciousness of freedom as our starting point, it will elucidate the meaning of his cosmic vision. I myself am responsible for my wretched state, and this guilt of mine implies a preexistential choice. It is the idea that I am free to rise or fall by my own activity that engenders the cosmic vision as a means of interpreting life. Freedom seemed to be a foreign element in the objective schema, but is actually its grounding principle. It is freedom that gives the schema truth and meaning.

My awareness that the present state of my soul is not final transcends existence and is explained by the origin of my soul: I did not spring from nothingness; rather, it was by my own will, before my time, that I fell into this condition; I still discern the workings of this will in motives which I experience in my present existence, motives which I do not identify with myself and from which, in my ascending movement, I strive to free myself.

Consequently Plotinus' vision of Being has two aspects which, though constantly merging, are essentially different. First, the eternal presence of the totality in its everlasting cycle, which lives and moves but changes nothing, and second, the fall and resurgence, in time, of individual souls through their own guilt and freedom. We must consider Plotinus' philosophy in the tension between on the one hand the eternity of Above-Being and Nonbeing, Spirit and world, and on the other hand the temporality of each soul's supersensory destiny.

With their conception of the creation and end of the world, Gnosticism and Christian theology drew being into the temporal process; they combated the doctrine that world and matter are eternal. Plotinus took the opposite step, raising the temporal world, considered as the intermediate realm of nature, above time. In his view the motion of the timeless whole is only apparent, while motion in nature is temporal. Entering into nature through its union with the body, the soul is caught up in temporal motion. Entering into the corporeality of the world, the soul became involved in fate. But something in the soul, its nucleus of eternal Being, remains intact, free from temporal motion. This eternal Being is forgotten but not extinct. Within the husk of the body, the soul enacts its fate, in which the recollection and reawakening of the center play a vital part. No decision is final. As low as the soul may fall, its center cannot die. A return is always possible. The soul has plenty of time, for the world is eternal.

Let us take a closer look at this view of fate and of the alternatives facing the soul.

A. *Necessity and freedom:* In Above-Being as the source of all things, there is neither necessity nor freedom. There is necessity in everything that comes after it. But is there also freedom? In current usage freedom means: what we do without constraint, what is done with our knowledge, and what is in our power. But Plotinus shows that mere process without constraint and in accordance with our nature is not free: if it were, uncontrolled fire would be free. Nor is happening with knowledge free, when I merely observe a process that would take place without me. Nor is what is in my power free, if it is done without right reflection and right striving. Nor is action free, for neither the conditions nor the situations nor the consequences of action are in our power.

Yet there is freedom: "Freedom does not depend upon act, but is a thing of the mind. Freedom in actions and free will pertain not to action but to inner activity, to the thinking and contemplation of virtue itself." Only reason (the *nous*) has "no master over it." It is possible only as freedom. "Freedom dwells in all those who conduct their lives according to reason and a rational striving." "The soul becomes free when through reason it strives unhindered toward the Good. Reason is free through itself." Freedom, for Plotinus, is inviolable. "God gave us virtue, subject to no master." The concept of freedom applies to that "which possesses the power of decision over itself" and to that which is distinct from "the existent that serves something other." Freedom is the best. The best begins with ourselves. "It is our nature when we are alone."

But freedom cannot mean that we make ourselves. "For it is impossible that something create itself and bring itself into being."

B. *Twofold guilt and twofold freedom:* "There is a twofold guilt for the soul." The one consists in the motive for the soul's fall from its supersensory home, the other in the crimes it commits here in the world. The soul atones for the first guilt by the sufferings it must bear in this world. It atones for the second by rebirth in other incarnations. To these two kinds of guilt correspond two kinds of freedom, the freedom of pretemporal choice and freedom of action in the world.

The mystery of pretemporal choice: "What caused souls to forget God the Father? . . . The beginning of evil for them was their overweening pride, the desire for change, the first otherness, and the craving to belong to themselves. Rejoicing in their own splendor, they forgot that they were descended from thence." They saw neither God nor themselves. From ignorance of their source, they did not honor themselves; they honored the Other and admired everything more than themselves.

Freedom in embodiment: Against Stoic determinism and the astrologers, Plotinus resolutely asserts our freedom. To be sure, Providence guides all things. But "Providence must not be such as to make us nothing." We try to blame Providence for the evil that accrues to the soul through its own guilt. Even if Providence subsequently transforms the soul's action into a link in the whole and so employs it for good ends, nevertheless, "the act of choice must be imputed to the soul." Man is not merely what he is in his earthly body. He is free in origin, but not outside the sphere of Providence.

c. *Evil:* Freedom itself is not evil. It becomes evil, not through something arising from within it, but through something other. We are not the source of evil; evil is anterior to us. "The evil that enters into men does not enter into them by their will; nevertheless, there is an escape from evil for those who are able, but not all men are able." This other, which is itself evil, is matter.

In answer to those who assert that matter is not evil, that "we should not seek evil in something other, but situate it in the soul itself," Plotinus declares that the soul, by definition, is life and hence good. It is not evil through itself.

Evil is a weakness of the soul. Weakness of the soul is not the same as weakness of the body. The cause of the soul's weakness, however, is not in itself, but in its bond with the body, whereby it has fallen into the corporeality of the world. And this weakness does not spring from a privation of something, but from the presence of something essentially different, matter.

Plotinus explains how this came about. Matter and soul occupy the same place. The soul inhabits a separate place only insofar as it does not dwell in matter. The soul could not have entered into a process of change except through the presence of matter. Soul and matter have merged into one. Matter is like a weight attached to the soul. The matter that dwells with the soul draws life from it and weighs it down; matter strives to penetrate the innermost core of the soul. The light emanating from the radiation of the soul is darkened and enfeebled by matter. The radiation of the soul was made possible by matter, for without matter the soul would not have descended. That is the "fall" of the soul: to have entered into matter and to have been enfeebled, to have been made evil by matter.

The consequences of an orientation toward matter spring from matter: freedom is limited. "Without a body, it is its very own master, free and outside of cosmic causes—drawn down into the body, it ceases to be in every way its own master. For its companion is governed largely by contingencies." Composition with the body makes the passions more violent, blunts the judgment, and gives rise to states of mind that vary according as we are hungry or satisfied. Through the material body the soul is easily aroused to desire, easily inclined to anger, overhasty in judgment, and surrenders readily to turbid imaginings, just as among the creatures the weakest succumb most readily to the wind or the heat of the sun.

To the argument that the soul should have mastered matter, Plotinus replies: The soul is not in a pure state, hence its power of mastery is diminished.

But the faculty of mastering matter is present. Freedom is not denied.

Hence, after the primal evil, the first evil, of matter, there is a second evil springing from weakness of the soul. The first evil is the disorder of matter, the second evil is that which becomes disorder by assimilation to matter, or participation in matter. The first evil is darkness, the second is that which is darkened. Consequently the soul obeys matter because of the second evil, but by virtue of its freedom it is able to govern the consequences of matter. "An inferior soul is driven to lust or anger; it becomes base in poverty, soft in wealth, tyrannical in the possession of power. . . . A good soul resists under all these circumstances." We can act "under the influence of outward forces, as though obeying a blind impulse." Then the soul is not free. "If on the other hand the soul follows reason, the pure, passionless, and authentic guide in its will, then such a will alone is free." Plotinus makes both statements: "Men are involuntarily evil, insofar as sin is involuntary." And: "It is the agent who acts, consequently it is he himself who sins."

The soul deteriorates in consequence of the fall. Once it has fallen into the body and been filled with matter, it remains in matter even when separated in death from its present body, "until the day when it rises upward and at some point averts its gaze from the muck." In consequence of an evil life the soul is re-embodied in an inferior form: one who has killed unjustly will be killed in another existence—unjustly as far as the agent is concerned, but justly so for the victim. What I do, I must suffer. The crime I inflict will be inflicted upon me. "For it should not be supposed that anyone is by chance a slave, or by chance taken prisoner. One who has slain his mother will himself become a woman in order to be killed by his son, and one who has violated a woman will himself become a woman and suffer the same fate." But transmigration is incidental in Plotinus. It is limited to the lower sphere, to natural existence.

D. *The two souls:* The fall and regeneration of the soul are seen in terms of "two souls"—a fundamental conception with Plotinus. The one soul is eternal, indestructible, and rational, remaining always in the intelligible world; the other is subject to change and suffering, bound to the body in the world; it approaches the first soul or moves away from it, and passes through many forms of existence. The second soul is suspended, as it were, from the first, like its shadow; projected into the body, it takes on corporeal existence; through the body it communicates with the sensory world. We are a twofold being; an animal has attached itself to our godliness. We carry the animal about with us.

The pure supersensory soul takes on the veils of spatiotemporal existence. But evil pertains only to existence, not to the soul. The soul is indestructible and merely changes its garment. "The changing souls become body now in this, now in that form; when it can, the soul departs from the world of change and remains at one with the world-soul."

In this world, however, the second soul suffers impurity. "Consider an ugly, unrighteous soul, full of unrest, craven fear, petty envy, forever occupied with base, transient thoughts, guileful, cringing in the byways, a lover of impure pleasures, wholly dependent on bodily influences, a soul that delights in ugliness: shall we not say that it has lost all purity of life and feeling, that mingled with evil it leads an impure life shot through with death, that it has ceased to behold what a soul should behold, that it cannot remain in itself, because it is perpetually drawn to the external, earthly, and dark?"

E. *The twofold longing:* The soul enters into the world, which partakes of nonbeing insofar as it is evil but is not absolute nonbeing. In the opposite direction, however, it attains not to something other, but to itself. It is itself in its association with the One. Only its primal ground perceives the primal ground, for like perceives like.

Driven by a twofold longing, the soul moves downward and upward. The moment it attains to the One, it falls away from the One. "As a chorus gathered round its leader may turn once again to look outward, but sings well and is truly in unison with him only when looking inward, so we too are always gathered round the One, but do not always look toward it; but when we do look, we are at the goal, we circle round it without discord in a chorus truly inspired by God."

Plotinus discerns all these motifs—the soul's twofold longing, its self-forgetfulness through the fall, its power to choose between the two directions—in the old myths. The fall of the soul is compared to young Dionysus looking into the mirror before being torn to pieces by the Titans. The bond with the body is the water of Lethe; drinking it, the soul forgets its true self. The soul allows itself to be carried away by nature: nature is Pandora, whom all the gods unite in decking out. Seeking the divine in the beauty of its own natural aspect, the soul is Narcissus, who flings himself into the pool while trying to embrace his reflection. In its twofold longing, for sensory beauty and eternal beauty, the soul is guided by a twofold Aphrodite, the one begotten by Uranus, the other by Zeus. The soul in the world is likened to Odysseus, who forsakes the carnal beauty of Circe and strives heavenward. And it is comparable to Herakles, who dwells now with the gods and now in Hades.

The soul rises through vision. Only from incapacity for vision, from weakness, does the soul, dissatisfied, turn to activity; it begins to make things in the hope of achieving what its Spirit could not. Thus "boys of lazy mind, incapable of philosophy, turn to crafts and skills."

But the vision of the soul is love and creation. By way of the eye the soul sees the visible forms of the beautiful. Loving, it perceives the imageless in the image, and gazing toward it attains peace and perfection. As the soul looks up at that which is above it, a copy of the archetype comes quietly into being, as though of its own accord; love is the artist.

But this twofold direction of longing introduces an ambiguity into love:

beauty guides physical generation. Though essentially inferior to heavenly love, earthly love is good, insofar as it derives reason from contemplation of the beautiful and the will to endure in time; it becomes evil only in decadence, in perversion, when without the image of the beautiful it is wholly oriented toward sensuality.

F. *The situation of the soul in the world:* The one eternal soul achieves its pure fulfillment in the spiritual world. "There it thinks; there it is without passions. And there alone is its authentic life; for its present life without God is only an echo of life." That is the life of gods and of divine, happy men, who have broken away from everything here below. But the "flight of the One to the One continues even beyond that blissful life."

The existence of two souls has an extraordinary consequence: the one soul is unaffected by all the evil in the world. Poverty and sickness mean nothing to good men, for the soul that has turned back from its self-forget-fulness is not touched by them. Yet like all evils, poverty and sickness benefit the wicked, for they punish and teach. Just as there is no good for the wicked, i.e., the self-forgetful soul that has descended to matter, so for the good there is no evil. The soul that has awakened to the One bears all the miseries of the world with patience, it attunes itself "to the natural law of the All." It was in the last period of his life, while desperately ill, that Plotinus wrote his moving tractate on Happiness.

"The Soul embarks with its tutelary spirit in the skiff of the universe. . . . The universal circuit is like a breeze, and a voyager . . . is carried forward by it. He has a hundred varied experiences, fresh sights, changing circumstances, all sorts of events. The vessel itself furnishes incident, tossing as it drives on." The Soul plays its appointed role in the cosmic drama (this great metaphor in Plato, the Stoics, Calderón, and the thinkers of India): "In the dramas of human art the poet provides the words, but the actors add their own quality, good or bad . . . and in the truer drama which dramatic genius imitates in its degree, the Soul displays itself in a part assigned by the Creator of the piece. As the actors of our stages get their masks and their costume, robes of state or rags, so a Soul is allotted its fortunes, and not at haphazard but always under a Reason: it adapts itself to the fortunes assigned to it, attunes itself, ranges itself rightly to the drama, to the whole Principle of the piece; then it speaks out its business, exhibiting at the same time all that a Soul can express of its own quality, as a singer in a song. A voice, a bearing, naturally fine or vulgar, may increase the charm of a piece; on the other hand, an actor with his ugly voice may make a sorry exhibition of himself, yet the drama stands as good a work as ever: the dramatist taking the action which a sound criticism suggests, disgraces one, taking his part from him, with perfect justice: another man he promotes to more serious roles or to any more important play he may have, while the first is cast for whatever minor work there may be."

This similarity between life and a role in a play determines the inner attitude of the man of insight: he does not complain of the particular role assigned him at birth. Nor does any reasonable man find fault with the other living creatures, which are beneath man but serve to beautify the earth. In considering the plants, we do not ask why they have no feeling, nor in considering the animals why they are not men. This would be as absurd as to ask why men are not the same as gods. "Universal equality there cannot be." The diversity of men is no ground for complaint; we do not find fault with a play "because its characters are not all heroes, but also include slaves and rustics."

A role has been assigned to us—let us play it well. This means that we should see the situation in the world and fulfill it. From the vast diversity of men, each man must draw the consequences for his role. For example: Men who are like irrational voracious beasts wish to do violence to others. The victims "are no doubt better than those who do them violence; if nevertheless they allow the wicked to defeat them, it is precisely because they themselves are evil in certain respects and not truly good." Our role demands that we fight for our own existence. Those who "from softness and indolence let the wolves tear them to pieces like fatted lambs" are visited with terrible sufferings for their inactivity. Since the world is governed by force, "not even a god will defend unwarlike men. The divine law decrees that those who fight bravely should be rescued from battle, not those who pray." Similarly, where work is called for, the harvest is reaped by those who till the soil, not by those who sit and pray. Would it not be absurd to follow our own opinion in all other matters, even in opposition to the gods, and then to expect the gods to save us? The gods gave us a commandment by which to save ourselves—we did not obey it. The wicked prevail because of their victims' unmanly conduct. Violence and war will be necessary as long as men do not truly contemplate the One, as long as they are not good. For Providence forbids that a world full of vices and unreason should obtain peace.

When Plotinus says: Fight, do not pray—does he mean to give action in the world precedence over vision? Not at all. Authentic vision is more powerful than action; but on the basis of his vision, a man should play his role in the world drama to the best of his ability; knowing his role, he should labor and do battle in accordance with it. But if he is in earnest, he will not be deceived. He will concern himself earnestly with earnest things, with vision, love, and ascent to the One. Playing his role, he will do battle, and not allow himself to be dominated by the wicked. But only those "who do not understand serious things, who are themselves playthings," play the role in earnest.

G. *Philosophy is ascent to the One:* Philosophy can find the upward path and travel it. It supplies a knowledge which in itself bears the soul upward.

The regeneration of the soul is accomplished first of all through ethos. The soul is purified by a philosophical way of life. "Without true goodness discourse on God is mere babbling." The good life is the presupposition as well as the consequence of philosophical thinking. A philosopher strives to depart from matter, from the body. But this flight is not a removal to an elsewhere in space; it is effected through the action of the rational soul in the world itself. There is no other means of flight from the world.

Given an ethical life, the soul can be purified by dialectic. But only the method can be taught. To follow it is the concern of the individual. "In speaking and writing, we employ concepts as a means of arousing the spirit to vision. For teaching shows the way; that is the beginning of the journey; but the actual seeing is up to the man who has made the decision to see."

Consequently the content of the doctrine is not in itself fulfillment. The doctrine of the One supplies only "analogies, negations, knowledge of its effects, and of certain degrees of ascent." Essentially, it provides a soul living in the world with two "demonstrations": it shows the vanity of the things it now prizes and reminds the soul of its origin and worth. These demonstrations are not logically compelling. They can succeed only if the soul becomes one with what it is investigating.

But not all earth-bound souls are equally capable of discerning their authentic being in the One. A soul must know "whether it has the power to undertake such an investigation, whether it has an eye capable of seeing. For if things are beyond its scope, what can its search avail? If it is bound to them in inner kinship, it will be able to find them." Plotinus was profoundly aware that we cannot adequately understand the teachings of philosophy with our reason, but only with our own being. Only our daily relation to ourselves and our memory of something that precedes all thought can kindle the meaning of philosophy within us; but once this happens, we in turn are magnified by our reflection on that meaning. In the temporal world the soul awakens to something that was already present within it. The soul in its embodiment is not a completed product which need only be examined to be known; its very being hinges on the freedom that seizes upon its potentiality. Refusal to seek ourselves in the ground of being is an assertion of our own emptiness. Those who say defiantly: I am what I am, cannot understand philosophy because they reject the possibility of an ascending movement.

Ascending thought is oriented toward the Supreme One: "the presence (*parousia*) that exceeds knowledge." "We must cast off all earthly veils, stand in this alone and become this alone." "Impatient with our fetters, we must hasten to escape from here." Hence the often repeated demand: "Let then him who can turn inward. Let him leave outside what the eye beholds, nor turn back to what formerly appeared to him as the radiance of corporeal beauty. For in beholding corporeal beauty, he must be aware that it discloses only contours and shadows, and flee to that of which it is the copy."

VII. AGAINST MATERIALISM AND GNOSIS

As beings of sense and understanding, we tend to think in terms of bodies and objects or not at all. We have then the choice of denying transcendence—as happens in materialism—or of transforming transcendence into a physical object with which to devaluate the real world—as in Gnosis. Plotinus defends his philosophy against both.

Against materialism for transcendence: There are men, says Plotinus, who look upon matter as the only true Being, the source of all things. That is the fault of appearance; to their mind bodies are Being. Troubled by the coming and going of corporeal forms, they conclude that Being is something underlying these bodies, which endures amid change. This something is matter.

Against the "enduring" as the characteristic of Being: Instead of regarding what somehow endures as Being, these thinkers should first have asked what the attributes of a true Being must be. A shadow, for example, remains present while the object changes, but it is not above the object in the scale of Being. If permanence were the hallmark of Being, we should have to rank space above bodies in respect to Being, because space is indestructible.

Against the primacy of matter in the sensory world: Those who have identified reality with matter have taken sense perception as their starting point, but they do not find matter itself in sense perception. All perceptible things are said to be merely the transient manifestation of imperceptible matter. "The astonishing part of it is that those who make sense perception the test of the true existence of all things, hold that Being cannot be apprehended by sense perception." Either they indicate characteristics of invisible matter that are perceptible to the senses (but when, for example they impute the power of resistance to matter, they are mistaken, for this too is a sensory quality like visibility, audibility, etc.), or else they try to explain matter by reason, which they go on to explain on the basis of matter. But is this not "an odd kind of reason, which gives matter precedence over itself and attributes being to matter rather than to itself"? What faith can one have in a reason which asserts its own nonbeing?

Imperceptible matter is conceived to be composed of atoms or elements (which are themselves formed matter). But the combination of atoms does not account for the qualities of things. Atoms and elements cannot be taken as the source of what is incommensurate with them, namely life, soul, spirit. An integral unity (e.g., the soul's unity of feeling) cannot be conceived as an aggregate of elements. What has no body, e.g., thought, memory, cannot spring from bodies.

Most untenable of all is the notion that the aggregate of atoms gave rise to things through chance. "Any attempt to derive order, reason, or the directing soul from the unordered motion of atoms or elements is absurd and impossible." Nothing in the world can be understood on the basis of matter alone. "For matter does not form itself, nor endow itself with soul. Thus there must be something else that leads the dance of life." Nothing would come into being, there would only be the nonbeing of matter if there were not some power to mold things and give them form. "Probably there would not even be matter and the All would disintegrate, were it dependent on the cohesive power of the corporeal."

Plotinus' critique of the materialists runs then as follows: If I see Being as such in sensible, corporeal presence, the diversity and instability of phenomena oblige me to conceive of something permanent underlying them. But if this something is matter, it is not accessible to sense perception. Such an operation of thought explains nothing. Matter alone can account neither for the diversity of phenomena, nor for the soul, nor for the thinking that thinks matter.

Plotinus adjures us to break with our tendency to find the reality of Being in matter. "Seek not therefore to see with mortal eyes such a thing as the One, the Spirit, the Soul." The prevailing opinion that all Being consists in the things of the senses must be abandoned, for it imputes the most Being to what has the most Nonbeing. Those who are unable to turn from the supposedly absolute reality of things to spiritual transcending will "remain bereft of the god like the gluttons who at feasts stuff themselves full of forbidden things, supposing these to be more substantial than contemplation of the god to whom the feast is dedicated. For also at these holy festivals (of philosophy) the invisible god causes those who rely only on what they see with the eyes of the flesh to doubt of his existence."

Against Gnosis in favor of the beauty of the world: Those who conceive the supersensory in corporeal terms and then, setting one body against another, reject the reality of the world are Gnostics. Their sensory vision of the supersensory blinds them to the real world of the senses. A spiritual vision of the supersensory, on the other hand, opens our eyes to the reflected radiance of the sensuous world. Plotinus justifies nature despite its low rank in the universal hierarchy and remoteness from pure being; in it he perceives the beauty of appearance.

The world is not Being. Those who condemn the world can do so only "because they do not know the hierarchical law extending from First to last." To condemn the world because of the many evil things in it means two things, first that we put too high a value on the world and second that we are blind to its true value as a copy. It is a mistake to expect the sensible world to resemble the intelligible world; let us recognize it, rather, as the best possible copy of the intelligible world.

Right vision of any particular being presupposes a vision of the whole. In the spiritual cosmos "all things are all, but not here below." Here in the world all things cannot be the same. For if they were, the mode of the world's being, the articulation and order of the whole in the separation of its parts, would be impossible. Thus the world as a whole is comparable to a living organism. Accordingly we should not ask whether one thing is inferior to another, but whether, taken as it is, it occupies its right place.

In a living organism "everything cannot be eye. The legs, the eyes, the mind do different things. We must not demand the same of things that are not alike. Seeing is not the concern of the finger. Each has its own function." Even the imperfect has its place. It is a mistake to condemn the whole because of the parts, as though in looking at a man we were to consider only a hair or a toe rather than the whole man.

The structure of the universe resembles that of the organism. In every living being the upper parts, the face and head, are more beautiful than the rest, the middle and lower parts do not resemble them. In the All, men are in the middle, above them heaven and its gods, below them the scale of living creatures extending down to the inanimate. Reason does not wish everything to be equally good, any more than an artist in painting an animal makes nothing but eyes. Reason does not people the All exclusively with gods, but divides it among gods, demons, men, and animals, each in turn, not out of envy, but because reason implies intellectual diversity.

The world is like a painting with its light and shadows; the shadows, too, contribute to its beauty. The world is not uniformity but a harmony of the dissimilar. Thus even evil is necessary in the world. If it were lacking, the whole would be incomplete.

The world discloses all things *in a process of change.* Every particular being is perishable. One thing limits and displaces another. All are engaged in a reciprocal war of annihilation. Through spatial separation diversity engenders hostility and makes friendship possible. "The part is not self-sufficient, it is preserved by something other, and is nevertheless hostile to that which preserves it. By its passing away one thing enables another to come into being." Each thing asserts itself in consequence of the will to live. The consequences are pain, suffering, death. "Living creatures devour one another, so that there is always war, which in all likelihood will never cease or end."

Not only must there be differences, but oppositions as well. As harmony arises from opposite tones, so the All accords with itself, while the parts battle one another. Reason derives its unity from conflicting concepts. "For if reason did not comprise multiplicity, it would not be a totality, it would be no reason at all." Because there is good, there must also be evil; because there is law and order, there must also be lawlessness and disorder.

Only particular beings perish. The world as a whole is eternal. "Perhaps it is necessary that beings devour one another in order that they may interchange and replace one another, for even if they were not killed, they could not endure forever. If they have benefited others, what ground is there for complaint?" "Destruction is not an evil to what has come into being through the death of something else; the fire that has been destroyed is replaced by other fire."

If in form the world resembles an organism, happening in the world is comparable to a drama. Death is a change of role. An actor murdered on the stage changes his costume and appears with another mask; in reality he has not died. "The conflicts among mortal men indicate that all human life is a game and show us that death is not bad, that by dying in war and struggle one anticipates a little what happens in old age, that one leaves the stage sooner in order to re-enter sooner. And as on a stage we must consider the murders, the different kinds of death, the conquest and pillage of cities, all as mere changes of scene, mere representations of sorrow and lamentation. For here too it is not the innermost soul that laments, but the outward shadow of the man."

All happening in the world is governed by a law. Everything in the world springs from reason and is therefore good, but at the same time everything is matter formed by reason and therefore bad. Because matter retains a certain power of Nonbeing, because everything is divided according to space and time, the necessity and contingency which result in disproportion and ugliness are everywhere present. But even these become in turn matter for the reason of Providence, which, though it did not will this matter, makes use of it once it has come into being, and integrates it with the rational context of the whole. "And this ability to make good use even of what is bad is proof of the highest power."

Providence exerts its irresistible guidance through inaction, which is more encompassing, deeper, and more powerful than action. The ability to do something with my own hands indicates that I lack something. Thus "the most godly are quite content to repose within themselves and to be what they are. To such men bustling activity would be dangerous, for it would take them out of themselves." In this sense the All is godly. Without action it accomplishes great things, precisely by resting in itself. The creation of the All was not planned. Unlike the human artist who works upon a material outside him, the world-soul makes no effort to produce anything. From its being the world arises spontaneously, without deliberation, for the spontaneity of the world-soul is above deliberation. "And so, quietly and without upheaval, the Spirit engendered the All by giving a fragment of itself to matter." Thus the All is a mixture of Spirit and Necessity (*anankē*). The world-soul "governs this All without effort, as though by its mere presence.

Viewing the whole, Plotinus says: "It is far better that beings and men live as if from the very beginning they had not come into being. For life would be impoverished by such a coming-into-being. But [without it] there is a rich life in the All, which incessantly produces beautiful and well-shaped playthings."

Plotinus lets the beautiful world speak for itself: "God created me, and I came from thence, perfect among all living beings, sufficient unto myself, needful of nothing, because everything is in me: plants and animals, many gods, multitudes of demons, good souls and men blessed with virtue. The earth is adorned with all manner of plants and animals, nor has the power of the soul stopped at the sea, leaving the air, the ether, and the heavens without a soul, for there dwell all the good souls that give life to the stars. Each thing within me strives toward the Good and each attains it according to its ability."

VIII. CRITICAL CHARACTERIZATION

A. *Contradictions:* Plotinus employs concepts that have two meanings, the one definable, the other serving to express the ineffable. Some of these are: vision (seeing, contemplation), the One, the Good, Being, the First, etc. Employed as means of thinking the unthinkable, they negate themselves and must be withdrawn. This structure—contradiction, tautology, vicious circle—is inevitable and appropriate when thought invites failure by trying to express what is beyond thought. Examples:

1. We are told that the One is attainable only through the negation of all determinations; however, numerous determinations, beginning with the "One" itself, are attached to it, often with the restriction "as it were." Similarly matter is denied all determination, yet Plotinus not only speaks of matter, but speaks of it in contradictory terms: matter is the counterpart of the Idea, the absolutely formless, and then again, considered as the last derivative, it is still, "in a manner of speaking, Idea."

2. A contradiction arises when individuality is considered first in opposition to the Idea and then as itself an Idea. On the one hand—and this is the dominant view in Plotinus—only the universal forms are Ideas, there is no Idea of the individual; there is an Idea of man, but not of Socrates. But on the other hand Plotinus says: "Individual men differ not only because of matter, but also by virtue of innumerable differences of form. They are not related to one another as the portraits of Socrates to their original." Their

difference springs rather from different primal forms. "Perhaps there are as many forms as there are different particular things, insofar as the difference does not rest merely on a lag behind the idea." "It need not frighten us that the number of forms is necessarily infinite."

3. Plotinus' conception of ascending and descending movement involves a contradiction inherent in the very nature of his philosophy.

The world is corruption and the world is miraculous beauty. Plato, says Plotinus, regarded the entire sensible world, especially the body, as an evil, as the prison or tomb of the soul; and then again, Plato in *Timaeus* called the world a blessed god, because it is endowed with soul, hence reason. Consequently the souls' descent into the world has a twofold aspect. Each individual soul is sent in order that the All may be complete; but each one is also guilty through an act of freedom. The soul is sent down to be a force in the beautiful world; at the same time, it has fallen through a pretemporal choice that ought not to have been made. It sprang from an original self-will, from pride and lust for change.

Both in the formation of the world as a whole and in the destiny of the individual soul, freedom and necessity are one. "Each soul has its own time: when that time comes, it descends as though at the call of a herald and enters into the body that is fit to receive it." It descends neither voluntarily nor under compulsion. Freedom is not to be understood as free choice, but is more "like" a natural drive, whether to mate or to perform heroic deeds. "There is no contradiction between the voluntary and the involuntary character of the descent." "In accordance with the eternal laws of its being," what it does freely, though "against its will," is necessary. What the soul takes upon itself redounds to the benefit of the body. "Its descent may be called a sending-down by God."

4. There is a contradiction in the concept of evil: Evil is only the less good, that which throughout the scale contains less Being; matter is absolute evil because it is Nonbeing. But elsewhere Plotinus departs from this negative concept and speaks of positive evil. Evil is only the shadow of the good, a necessary part of the total harmony; it is mere deficiency and nothing in itself; and then again it is an active power of seduction, man's subservience to which is the "second evil."

5. Plotinus' concept of the divine is equally contradictory. God is the One, yet there are many gods. The One dominates all Plotinus' thinking, but he reveres more than one god.

All these contradictions seem meaningful when Plotinus' vision of Being is considered as a whole. Where he himself notices them, he overcomes them by his doctrine of degrees or by his knowledge of the inadequacy of speech. To disclose them is more to elucidate the philosophy of Plotinus than to criticize it.

B. *Empirical knowledge and mythical conceptions:* Plotinus' indifference to the world prevents him from taking any interest in natural science. He does not inquire into the particulars of nature, because he is concerned only with the One. Consequently he takes over unquestioningly the mythical conceptions of his time and its barbaric notions of science. He recognizes demons and love magic.

But Plotinus was a man of natural good sense. In connection with the nature of disease, astrology, demonological healers, etc., he expresses certain critical doubts. He attacks the thaumaturges who "hypostasize diseases as demonic beings" and the populace who let themselves be impressed by their supposedly miraculous powers: "They will never convince anyone who thinks clearly that diseases are not caused by overexertion, too much or too little food, and processes of putrefaction."

But both the mythical-magical conceptions and the good sense apply only to the subordinate world of nature, which is of no importance to men of wisdom. This is the realm of material influences on the body-bound soul. Those who would rather be guided by sensory experience than by philosophy can also resort to oracles. But a man rises to the truth only by thinking, that is, by immersion in the depths of his own soul and spirit, not through the gods. That is why Plotinus takes no more interest in magic and astrology than in empirical investigation and knowledge. All these fields of knowledge occupy a low rank. Yet in dealing with them he shows the "simplicity of character, combined with pure and clear thinking," to which he aspired in all his philosophizing.

Plotinus excluded science and politics from his philosophy. The stream of the world process, springing from the One and returning to the One, is ahistorical, pure actuality. The soul achieves self-certainty and transcendence by thinking this one vast cipher of being. Plotinus is the purest and most exclusive of metaphysicians.

c. *The existential meaning:* Let us attempt a deeper characterization of Plotinus' philosophy. In it the soul gains awareness that its core is intangible, indestructible, and immortal, and this is what gives him his wonderful serenity. If the soul can know and unfold its pure essence, nothing in the world can affect it.

Such serenity is possible, because the soul knows its home to be elsewhere. Beholding the source of all things, it gains contentment in its intuition of universal harmony.

But this contentment is that of an onlooker. The soul is twofold, affected by sufferings, but in its innermost core unaffected, as a participant in the world, involved in its torments, as an onlooker untouched. A wise man, Plotinus quotes, is happy, even when slowly burned in the glowing bronze bull of Phalaris. The harmony of the whole is not disturbed by the disharmony of the individual: Plotinus speaks of the "men who are the joy of God, who bear all the miseries of the world with patience, even when through the cyclical motion of the All they are afflicted with a necessary evil. For our attention must be directed not at the desires of the individual, but at the interest of the whole."

Such contentment seems questionable. Harmony is found in a theoretical vision of the whole and in the many beauties of the world; the particular evil is not interpreted and taken into account. Is this not to ask the impossible of men? Can a man overwhelmed by suffering content himself with the harmony of the whole if this harmony is not manifested in his actual life? Who benefits by the concrete harmony which demands this terrible present suffering? In order to believe in this harmony must I not deliberately delude myself?

It is possible no doubt to bear physical suffering with equanimity, but even that is contingent on my physical and mental constitution; it ceases to be possible when suffering impairs my consciousness. Even a "wise man" would not reject the modern techniques of easing pain.—But what of the sufferings that come with the crises of life, when the whole world pales to nothingness, or the torment arising from guilt, or seemingly hopeless solitude, or a friend's betrayal? Where such sufferings are ignored, the question of suicide loses its depth. The only motive recognized by Plotinus is anger, an impure passion. Plotinus asks whether a man is justified in taking his life if he feels that his mind is failing. His answer shows his tendency to smooth over the difficulties of existence: "Perhaps that will not happen to a wise and virtuous man." But if it does, suicide is to be counted among "necessary" actions, those to which we are driven by the course of nature, which are justified under certain circumstances, but not in any absolute sense. For Plotinus mental disorder was not a problem. Altogether we must question this serenity of the onlooker who accepts the sufferings of the innocent and all the recurrent injustice of the world as a necessary part of the universal harmony.

Is Plotinus blind to the realities which directly conflict with any idea of harmony? He is unwilling to consider evil as a positive power; it is mere deficiency, mere Nonbeing (and yet in the course of his thinking he is sometimes compelled to recognize a positive evil). Anyone who ponders the undeniable sufferings and injustices of the world cannot but rebel against the Plotinian "peace in harmony."

In becoming a mere change of scene, *death* loses its sting. And this present life loses its weight as the unique and only life. The eternal soul has entered into this life as into one of many successive roles, its core is unaffected. If it lives badly, it has the possibility of purification after death, in new forms of existence. Both life and death lose their earnestness.

With this devaluation of our worldly existence and death, the particular circumstances of life become indifferent. Bodily pain, mental torment, loss of the necessities of life, "destruction of the city," death of our loved ones— all become meaningless appearance. Nothing in the world has absolute importance. Only those lacking in wisdom can concern themselves seriously with the world.

The extreme situations which awaken man, but which, even after they have brought home to him the earnestness of his existence and made transcendence a reality for him, never lose their real power to call everything into question all over again, are veiled or spirited away by Plotinus' vision of universal Being. Since fundamentally all problems raised by such a vision are solved in advance, they lose their power. Such a system is a closed circle: the belief in harmony annuls the extreme situations, while insensibility to extreme situations makes possible the belief in harmony.

All real danger ceases with the experience of worldless transcendence, which is repeated over and over again in speculation. This speculation confers a benign sense of security; it does not penetrate the world, but accepts it passively and without trying to understand it. Hence Plotinus' serenity, his tranquil radiance. In this realm there is no quarreling and no despair.

The individual and his individual interests become matters of indifference. Peace will descend when I as myself vanish; I gain insight in union with the One, when subject and object vanish.

Even though Plotinus sometimes asserts the uniqueness of the human individual, all his categorial thinking presupposes the pre-eminence of the universal: the individual is unknowable but also unimportant. For matter is the principle of individuation (even as intelligible matter, it is the principle underlying the diversity of the eternal forms). With Plato, Plotinus holds that "the unity of Being is fragmented *ad infinitum.*" The lowest class, which cannot be subdivided into further classes, is infinite and, once relegated to infinity, ceases to be of interest. The individual is without interest, because it has no Being in the sense of the universal, the *eidos,* but owes his infinity to matter.

Because the individual is without importance, Plotinus has no mind for history. He demands, to be sure, that man should play his role in the world, but here he envisages mere action without inner participation: the world is robbed of its significance as unique realization. Plotinus does not take up his destiny in the awareness that he can gain substance only as a historical being. He is not awake to the significance of absolute decision in time, of a historical happening that can bring the certainty of authentic being. Whatever happens, the soul is immortal and can make atonement in new forms of existence; whatever is done can be undone.

Thus Plotinus' conception of freedom is not grounded in action in the world. He does not know the unity of time and eternity. For the historical consciousness, the eternal is decided in time; the things of the world are phenomenal and at the same time infinitely important; the world is the only medium in which being is disclosed; there is no such thing as flight out of the world. This paradoxical union of time and eternity is unknown to Plotinus. In his view the world is a mere stage, my life is only a role. No decision I can make carries the weight of eternity. There is only a rising and falling, the possibilities remain always the same. Nothing in the world is really serious, the only thing that counts is purity of soul—and this purity is situated in an innermost core, inaccessible to the world, which finds fulfillment in incommunicable ecstasy.

Because the individual is without importance, Plotinus' conception of love, directed toward the One, seems at once grandiose and empty. Our love should be directed at the simple and absolute, not at anything partial and contingent. We must see the beautiful as such, "not any of its finite embodiments." That the "contingent," "partial," "finite" are the manifestation of an existence which is always historical, whose essential being is distilled in the crucible of loyalty and integrity—such an idea is alien to Plotinus. The impersonal love of the One deprives marriage and friendship of their meaning. Plotinus' love does not grow into the substance of the soul through existential decision in an irreplaceable historical context; it merely contemplates the eternal forms in degrees ranging from the generative power of nature to union with the One.

Thus it is characteristic of Plotinus that he should reject every indication of the individual's historical substance or social setting. He declines to speak of his own parents or origin. He refuses to love any woman, for "there are no marriages in heaven." He cares nothing for political existence and is unaware of its historicity. He does not know the profound meaning of political action as an always unique process, to which the individual contributes with his freedom.

Because Plotinus is indifferent to the irreplaceable individual, because he transfers love from the real world to transcendence, because he dismisses the earnestness of historical decision from his purview and concentrates on an intangible eternal self beyond all worldly reality, transcendence and the immortal soul become punctual abstractions in his thinking. They are ciphers rich in potential meaning that can be fulfilled only through existence in the world.

Plotinus' vision of the harmonious whole, his indifference to the temporal roles played by men, his passionate striving for purity of soul, his experience of transcendence in thinking toward the unthinkable, which in supreme moments anticipates union with the One—all these leave a strangely mixed impression. They carry the ring of manifest truth, and yet one cannot help wondering: Is this ultimate peace not a serene death in life?

Plotinus soars magnificently to the One, from the unity of things in the world to the One itself in transcendence, from unity in the beauty of a particular living being to the sublime beauty of the All and beyond the beauty of the soul to the ground of the One itself. But all this is pure contemplation. Lacking are the other meanings of the One, which would give such contemplation practical efficacy: the One in historical fulfillment of the one idea I serve; the one love, in which I become myself or lose myself; the transcendent One, which in the ciphers of thought remains ambiguous, and achieves self-certainty only in practice. In order to pass from potentiality to reality, I must become existentially one, objectively limited in time, which through the One becomes historical. In Plotinus' life practice the necessary One is only the soul's ascent to the One; "the goal must be one and not many; otherwise, we should seek not a goal but goals."

The limitations of Plotinus' philosophy become apparent in epochs when action in the world is essential, when the individual takes on importance, when history speaks as the presence of the eternal, when extreme situations are taken seriously.

IX. HISTORICAL POSITION AND INFLUENCE

Plotinus believed his ideas to be those of Ammonios Saccas, his teacher in Alexandria. But Ammonios the man has no place in Plotinus' writings, and we know next to nothing about him. It is Plato, not Ammonios, whose presence we feel in Plotinus' philosophizing. He also speaks of Aristotle, the pre-Socratics, and the Stoics. He thought in the forms laid down in the philosophical tradition of the schools, but shattered their content, not out of polemical destructiveness but because he was obsessed by the supersensory One, an idea that he developed in full purity and with all its consequences. On the surface, his work may seem to be a combination of traditional (Platonic, Aristotelian, Stoic) elements. Actually they are transformed by a process of transcending that had never before been carried out so persistently and radically. Unlike Heraclitus and Parmenides, Plotinus had the concepts of the intervening Greek philosophers to work with. He was not a creator; he refashioned existing concepts into a great, new, self-contained unity. And he was conscious of repeating the ancients, especially Plato. "These ideas are not new; they were stated long ago, though not clearly and sharply. The present ideas are interpretations of those old ideas."

Plotinus knew how close he was to Plato. For Plato had elucidated the transcendence of the One (in the notion of "Beyond-Being") in his negative theology, and in his derivation of the world from unity and Being in the first and second "hypotheses" of the *Parmenides*. But he was also very different from Plato. An operation which Plato carried out with playful inventiveness and regarded as merely one factor in his dialectical philosophy became for Plotinus the exclusive absolute. Plato looked upon philosophizing as an activity through which man comes to *resemble* the divine, and never thought of bridging the gulf between them; for Plotinus philosophizing was a *union* with the divine, whereby the distance between man and God was annulled. Plato observed a dividing line between world and transcendence; Plotinus crossed it. Plato carries out transcending movements in human existence; Plotinus lives in the one transcendence. In a playful tale.

Plato invents a world-architect, a demiurge; Plotinus makes everything issue from the One. Although Plotinus quotes Plato literally in support of his own central ideas, he is actually drawing on a very different source to establish an all-pervading metaphysical way of life.

With incomparable devotion Plotinus seized upon the idea of God explicitly formulated by Xenophanes, meditated upon by Parmenides (without being called God) and by Plato, which in Aristotle had degenerated into a logical construction and in Stoicism into pantheism. This was the philosophical idea of God.

Plotinus drew on the cosmology of Poseidonius (c. 135–50 B.C.), who in turn had taken his view of nature from Plato's *Timaeus*. But there is an essential difference between the two systems: in the Stoic materialism of Poseidonius the transcendent One is lacking; his world-reason is the fiery pneuma, consubstantial with the human spirit, while Plotinus transcends spirit as well as matter. In Poseidonius there is not so much as a suggestion of what students of Plotinus have always found so deeply moving.

In those days there was a body of thought associated with the Mysteries, Orphic ideas, and Oriental lore. The form it assumed in the period of Plotinus is known as Gnosis. In the Gnostic conception, the soul has a heavenly home from which it has fallen. It is wrapped in veils that conceal it from itself. It longs to be gone from the illusion, impurity, and evil of this existence and return to its home. The true life is the life which enables the soul to find the way back. In its fall the soul is clothed in foreign substance, which it casts off in returning upward. The cosmos is the scene of these journeys, whose successive stations constitute its geography.

This schema is one of the backgrounds of Plotinus' thinking. But Plotinus opposed Gnosticism with its materialized stages and its redeemer sent by the transcendent God, who guides the soul upward from this world created by an evil being. His purpose is purely philosophical, the self-liberation of the individual soul; he acknowledges the splendor of this world, and rejects both the Gnostic conception of a temporal history of Being and the fanciful multiplication of intermediate stages which later Neoplatonists took over from the Gnostics.

Quite apart from the vagueness of such historical concepts as "Oriental" and "Greek," the thesis that Oriental thinking invaded Greek philosophy with Plotinus must be rejected. The dignity of the human personality, which through thinking achieves awareness of its independence, is an effective force in Plotinus. He is moved by the beauty of the cosmos. He revered the "divine Plato" and the ancient philosophers from Parmenides and Heraclitus to Aristotle. The Greeks had been subject to Oriental influence since the earliest times. In assimilating it, they transformed it, giving speech to something which without them would have remained mute. This is also true of Plotinus, who from early youth was passionately interested in the wisdom of India and the Orient.

When we consider the philosophical life of his day, we can only agree with Dodds that amid Philo's theosophical dreams, Tertullian's poisoned fanaticism, Porphyry's amiable pieties, and the unspeakable inanities of the Mysteries, Plotinus alone has the appeal of a true thinker; that he rejected Gnosis and theurgy and resolutely raised the claim of reason as instrument of philosophy and key to the structure of reality.

Both in his being and in his achievement, Plotinus was above his times. Under the Emperor Gallienus, to be sure, art experienced a "renaissance," which was also the swan song of ancient classicism; but it is a far cry from this sculpture, whose interest today is purely historical, to the philosophy of Plotinus, which is an eternal monument of Western culture.

It would be mistaken to interpret the attitude of Plotinus as a weariness reflecting the dying civilization of his age. Quite the contrary, his life and thinking are an example of the irresistible vigor of philosophy. But his thinking does have the power to help people in overcoming their world-weariness.

Plotinus' influence down to our own day has been extraordinary. He is the father of all "speculative mysticism," surpassed by none of its later representatives. His influence is remarkable for its depth and also for the distortions it has undergone.

Plotinus is regarded as the founder of "Neoplatonism." He lived in the third century, Iamblichus in the fourth, Proclus in the fifth, Damascius and Simplicius in the sixth century. But "the influence of Plotinus' original text on the Neoplatonists is almost non-existent. Actual quotations are rare" (Harder). Plotinus' successors did not derive from his spirit. They were chiefly interested in restoring pagan religion, in transforming the figures of the philosophers into saints, in founding a philosophical religion. They were given to undisciplined flights of fancy. At the same time, they developed a philosophical scholarship some of whose achievements are still highly valued, and some of them were extraordinary teachers of philosophy.

Plotinus was also taken over by Christian thinkers, above all by Augustine. Here the philosophical source was negated. Plotinus' transcendent One was manifest to reason; the Christian God manifested Himself through Christ. The new philosophy was based, not on philosophical inquiry as such, but on faith in a unique revelation. Plotinus' Above-Being was degraded to Being, the spiritual cosmos was elevated to become God's thoughts. The two merged and became a personal God. Plotinus' three hypostases (the One, Spirit, the World-Soul) were replaced by the Trinity; Plotinus' emergence of all being, by the Creation and the mysterious relations between the members of the Trinity.

In Neoplatonism the materialization of Plotinian thinking found its most impressive representative in Proclus (410–485). The ideas of Proclus were taken up in the writings of Pseudo-Dionysius Areopagita (c. 500), through whom they became an element in all medieval thinking. Plotinus himself achieved new influence with the Renaissance (Marsilius Ficino, 1433–1499).

A misunderstanding fraught with enormous consequences was the identification of Plotinus with Plato. Long seen as a kind of Plotinus, Plato was rediscovered step by step. Finally, in the course of the last hundred years, he became visible as himself. It was only then that an understanding of Plotinus' own characteristic greatness became possible.

LAO-TZU

LIFE AND WORKS

The story of Lao-tzu's life is told by Ssŭ-ma Ch'ien (c. 100 B.C.). He was born in the state of Ch'u, in the present province of Honan in northern China. For a time he was state archivist (historian) for the central government, the Chou emperor. He did his best to live in obscurity and to remain nameless. At an advanced age, when conditions in his home state of Ch'u became intolerable, he journeyed westward. At the behest of the border guard he wrote the *Tao Tê Ching,* in five thousand words. Then he vanished into the West. "No one knows where he ended his life." Chuang-tzu says, however, that Lao-tzu died at home, surrounded by his scribes. He is said to have lived in the sixth century B.C. (the traditional view, for this alone would make possible the conversations between him and Confucius, which others put down as legendary), but other traditions place him in the fifth (Forke) or even the fourth century. The question will probably never be settled with any degree of certainty. His name is mentioned neither by Confucius nor by Mencius nor by Mo Ti. In view of the state in which the literature of that greatest century of Chinese culture has come down to us, it seems doubtful, at least to an outsider, whether Sinologists will ever succeed in dating the *Tao Tê Ching* accurately by comparing its style with that of other texts. The dating is unimportant for the interpretation of the text. The discussions on the subject merely bear witness to the uncertainty of the tradition.

The authorship of the *Tao Tê Ching* and the authenticity of certain parts have been contested. However, its inner cohesion is so convincing that— despite possible interpolations and distortions—one cannot doubt that it was created by a thinker of the highest rank. The man seems to stand before us and speak to us.

Tao Tê Ching, the Book of *Tao* and *Tê,* is a work of maxims of varying length, divided into eighty-one short chapters. The arrangement follows no one system. Sometimes, as toward the end of the "political" section, there are groups of connected chapters. The essential is stated at the very beginning and then recurs in richly meaningful amplifications. Although there is no argumentative development, only aphoristic statement of the complete thought, repetition of the same idea in numerous modifications gives a magnificent impression of consistency. Without systematic terminology, there is a unity of thought which lends itself to systematic interpretation. The power of its paradoxical formulations (without playfulness or irresponsible wit), its earnestness, and the impact of a seemingly unfathomable depth make the book one of the irreplaceable works of philosophy.

A layman can study the text only by comparing the numerous translations and their commentaries. We cannot read Lao-tzu as we read Kant, Plato, or Spinoza. The text does not speak to us directly in its own language, but through a medium which clouds and muffles it—or on occasion sets it off in too glaring a light. The differences in meaning between one translation and another are sometimes enormous, quite particularly in Chapter 6: according to de Groot it deals with regulation of the breath, in other translations with the root of the universe, the "spirit of the valley," or the "underlying womanly"; according to Lieh-tzu, to be sure (Strauss), the whole chapter is a quotation from an older book; Lao-tzu was in the habit of quoting lines of poems, songs, and hymns. The reader is advised to make use of several translations. The figures designate chapters of the *Tao Tê Ching*.

An understanding of Lao-tzu is facilitated by a knowledge of Chinese thought, of the age in which he lived, of earlier traditions. If we are able here to dispense with a historical introduction, it is because of the timeless character of this metaphysical thinking, which seems especially true and moving when considered apart from its historical setting.

I. EXPOSITION OF LAO-TZU'S PHILOSOPHY

Tao is the origin and goal of the world and all things, hence also of the thinker. The philosophy tells us first, what Tao is; secondly, how all being proceeds from it and moves toward it; thirdly, how man lives in Tao, how he can lose it and regain it, both as an individual and in a political society.

Thus in Western terms, it deals with metaphysics, cosmogony, ethics, and politics. In Lao-tzu all these are one in the all-pervading fundamental idea. In a single short chapter all four elements can appear at once. While in an exposition we must differentiate these factors and treat them successively, in the book as in the philosophy they are one fundamental idea. An exposition can be considered successful if it conveys an awareness of this fundamental unity.

1. *The Tao*

Penetrating to the remotest depths, the book begins: "The Tao that can be told of is not the eternal Tao; the name that can be named is not the eternal name. The Nameless is the origin of Heaven and Earth" (1). In these lines the author declares not only all over-hasty knowledge, but in general the mode of knowledge with which man approaches finite things, to be inapplicable to the Tao. "I do not know its name; I call it Tao" (25).

If we are to speak of it, it can only be in negative statements (as in saying that it is unnamable, that is, inaccessible to human naming). For example: "We look at it and do not see it; Its name is The Invisible. We listen to it and do not hear it; Its name is The Inaudible. We touch it and do not find it; Its name is The Subtle (formless)" (14).

Any attempt to express its being in positive terms reduces it to the finite. "Tao is empty (like a bowl)" (4); it is the infinite abyss; "It may be used, but its capacity is never exhausted" (4). If we name it, grasp it, understand it, if we attempt to differentiate it in our thinking or to see distinctions in it, it vanishes: "It reverts to nothingness" (14). Its original fullness is more than any fullness we can comprehend, its shapelessness is more than any shape we can understand. "This is called shape without shape, form without objects. It is The Vague and Elusive. Meet it and you will not see its head. Follow it and you will not see its back" (14).

What for us becomes an object is finite: for us differentiation and definition constitute being. A rectangle is by virtue of its angles, a vessel by virtue of its content, an image by virtue of its form. But when an object becomes infinite and undifferentiated like the Tao, it loses its distinctness, ceases to be what it was when differentiated. Thus to think of an object that has become infinite can guide us to the thinking of the Tao; Lao-tzu says: "The great square has no corners. The great implement (or talent) is slow to finish (or mature). Great music sounds faint. Great form has no shape" (41).

Insofar as being is what we see, hear, and grasp, insofar as it is image and form, Tao is nothing. Only in the Tao that is free from being is the source attained. This source is not nothing in the sense of not-at-all, but in the sense of more-than-being, whence come existing things: "And being comes to nonbeing" (40).

Nonbeing is the source and aim of all being. In itself it is essential being and as such beyond being. After such statements by negation about this nonbeing a load of seemingly positive statements is put upon it. Tao is unchanging. "It depends on nothing and does not change" (25). It does not age (30, 55). Tao is dependent on itself, while man, earth, heaven, and all things outside of the Tao are dependent on something else (25). Tao is simple (32, 37), it is still (25), it is undifferentiated yet complete in its repose (25).

But the repose of Tao cannot be the opposite of motion; for then it would be merely negative, less than being. Tao moves, but in motion it is at the same time at rest; its motion is "reversion" (40). It moves, but not because it wishes to attain something that it is not and has not, for Tao is without need, "without desires" (34, 37).

In Lao-tzu's day Tao was already a traditional concept. The original meaning of the word was "Way"; then it came to mean the order of the cosmos and, what was seen as identical, the right conduct of man. It has been translated as reason, *logos,* God, meaning, right way, etc. It has even been interpreted as a personalized deity, either female or male.

Lao-tzu gave the word a new meaning. He used it as a name for the ground of all being, although the ground of being is as such nameless and unnamable. Using this word, he transcended everything that was called being, including the universe, and even the Tao as cosmic order. He retained, to be sure, the concept of cosmic being and the idea of its all-pervading order, but both of these are rooted in the transcendent Tao.

Tao antecedes the world, hence antecedes all differentiation. It can neither be confronted with anything else nor can it be in itself differentiated. In it, for example, what is and what ought to be are identical; things that are separate and opposed in the world are one before the world; identical are the law according to which everything happens and the law according to which everything ought to happen; identical are the order that has been from all eternity and the order that remains to be ushered in by true ethical action. But this unity of opposites cannot at the same time be a particular reality in the world nor can it be the whole of the world. It remains the source of the world and the goal of the world. To become world means to separate and to be differentiated, it means cleavage and opposition.

For us the multiplicity of things in the world results from separation and opposition. Tao is called empty, because it is undifferentiated, without object, without opposition, because it is not world. In fulfilling itself, Tao posits objects, produces the world. But Tao itself is never filled in this way (4). If it could be filled by the created world, it would become one with it. In emptiness it remains—we are justified in interpreting—richer in potentiality than all mere reality in the world, in nonbeing it is more than being, in the undifferentiated ground greater than all determinate, objectively differentiated being. It remains the Encompassing.

2. *Tao and world*

It was before Heaven and Earth came into being (25); it was even before Ti, the Lord on High, the supreme god of the Chinese (4). But Tao is not something inaccessible and totally other, it is present. Imperceptible, it can nevertheless be experienced as the true being in all being. Present in all things, it is that from which all things, whatever they may be, derive their being. The *signs* of its presence in the world are:

A. *It is present as nonbeing:* Eye, ear, hand seek the Tao in vain, but it is everywhere. "The Great Tao flows everywhere" (34). It is comparable to the tangible nonbeing through which all determinate being is: just as the utility of the vessel depends on the empty space which it contains and the utility of the house depends on the emptiness of doors and windows (11). Thus the nothingness of Tao is the nonbeing that first gives things being.

It is comparable to something that would permeate even the most massive and unporous body: "Nonbeing penetrates that in which there is no space" (43). Because it is like nothingness, no existing thing resists it. "Though its simplicity seems insignificant, none in the world can master it" (32). "It operates everywhere and is free from danger" (25).

B. *It acts as though not acting:* "Tao invariably takes no action, and yet there is nothing left undone" (37). It acts imperceptibly as though powerless. "Weakness is the function of Tao" (40). Tao is infinitely active because it produces all things, but it acts with discreet quietness that does nothing.

Although Tao is the superior power that produces all things, it leaves all things free, as though each thing were what it is not through Tao but through itself. Hence the worship of Tao is instilled in all beings by their origin, but each being is left free to worship according to his own essence: "Tao is worshiped not by command but spontaneously" (51). Tao brings about the free compliance of beings: "For it is the way of Heaven not to strive but none the less to conquer; not to speak but none the less to get an answer; not to beckon; yet things come to it of themselves" (73).

Tao is able to move beings without constraint because it makes itself disappear in their presence, as though it did not act and had never acted. It "produces but does not appropriate, it acts but does not rely (on the result), and raises (beings) without lording it over them" (51). "It accomplishes its task, but does not claim credit for it. It clothes and feeds all things but does not claim to be master over them" (34).

Working irresistibly, it conceals its irresistible nature; it humbles itself and blends with the surroundings: "It blunts its sharpness, subdues its brilliance, becomes one with its dust" (4).

C. *Tao is the source of the One within all oneness:* All things have being insofar as they are held by the bond of oneness, of the One, which is the productive form of the Tao, not one as a number, but Oneness as essence. "Of old those that obtained the One: Heaven obtained the One and became clear. Earth obtained the One and became tranquil. The spiritual beings obtained the One and became divine. The valley obtained the One and became full. The myriad things obtained the One and lived and grew. Kings and barons obtained the One and became rulers of the empire" (39).

D. *All existence derives its being from Tao:* "It is bottomless, perhaps the ancestor of all things!" (4). "It may be considered as the mother of the universe" (25). All things owe their preservation to this father—or mother. "Tao gave them birth; the power of Tao reared them . . . developed them"

(51). Without Tao all things are lost; but "it does not turn away from them" (34). "The essence is very real; in it are evidences" (21).

E. *Tao is beyond good and evil but is infinitely helpful:* All beings without exception, both good and evil, have their being through Tao; in it they have their foundation, hence a kind of permanence. "Tao is the storehouse of all things. It is the good man's treasure and the bad man's refuge" (62).

Though termed love, faith, reliability, Tao is not moved by human compassion, it prefers no one and does not take sides. This is shown in the image of the cosmos; the coming and going of all things is endless and vain: "How Heaven and Earth are like a bellows! While vacuous, it is never exhausted. When active, it produces even more" (5). The cosmos is indifferent to individuals: "Heaven and Earth are not humane. They regard all things as straw dogs" (5). "The Way of Heaven has no favorites. It is always with the good man" (79). "The Way of Heaven is to benefit others and not to injure" (81).

Thus the principal signs of the existence of Tao in the world were all-pervading nonbeing, the imperceptible nonaction that accomplishes all things, the all-producing power of oneness, the power beyond good and evil which sustains the beings "that come and go."

Cosmogony and the process of the individual in the world

Lao-tzu strives to go beyond his vision of Tao in the world to the cosmogonic process, to the riddle: Why did the world spring from Tao? But he merely hinted at such speculation, he did not develop it constructively. He did not ask why the world is. Nor did he ask how things strayed from the right path. He seems to know of no cosmic process in time, marked by a series of crucial founding events or catastrophes. One would tend rather to infer from his sayings a timeless eternal presence as the fundamental essence of being. The hints at a cosmic process that occur in Lao-tzu should perhaps be interpreted as an eternal becoming.

A. *There are two Taos, which were originally one:* First the Tao that is not namable, nonbeing, and secondly, the Tao that can be named, or being. The unnamable Tao is called "origin of Heaven and Earth," the namable is called the "mother of the ten thousand things" (1). This "mother" is being: "All things in the world come from being" (40); nonbeing has no name: "And being comes from nonbeing" (40). The Tao is not namable as such but only as manifested in being. The emergence of things from the namable Tao is itself the ever-recurring genesis of the namable: "As soon as Tao begins to create and to order, it has a name. Once the block is carved there will be names, and as soon as there are names they will be known" (32).

Both the unnamable and the namable Tao, nonbeing and being, "are the same, but after they are produced, they have different names" (1). Viewing the unnamable through the namable, thought penetrates to the unfathomable: "They both may be called deep and profound" (1).

Elsewhere the cosmogonic process is outlined as follows: "Tao produced the One. The One produced the two. The two produced the three. And the three produced the ten thousand things. The ten thousand things carry the *yin* and embrace the *yang,* and through the blending of the material force they achieve harmony" (42).

B. The productive Tao bears within it the elements of being, which may be conceived of as forms, images, substances, or forces: "Eluding and vague, in it are things. Deep and obscure, in it is the essence. The essence is very real; in it are evidences" (21).

c. Within the cosmic process the process of the individual is contained. The motion of beings in the cosmos seems to be of two kinds: a futile coming and going from nothingness to nothingness or a return home to the source: "All things flourish, but each one returns to its root. This return to its root means tranquillity. It is called returning to its destiny. To return to destiny is called the eternal (Tao)" (16).

3. *Tao and the individual (ethics)*

"The All-embracing quality of the great virtue follows alone from the Tao" (21). High virtue, authentic life (*tê*), is unison with Tao. Only with Tao can man follow the right path. Thus the salient characteristics of the Tao—action through nonaction, being through nonbeing, strength through softness—will reappear in the True Man.

But man does not, like nature, follow the Tao by necessity: man can fall away from Tao; most men have already done so, but they can again become one with the Tao.

A. *The fall from Tao: intention and self-striving:* The original fall from Tao is self-striving, which is identical with intention in action, hence with self-reflection, with zeal, and with purposive bustle.

"The man of superior virtue is not (conscious of) his virtue, and in this way he really possesses virtue. The man of inferior virtue never loses (sight of) his virtue, and in this way he loses his virtue" (38). In other words, what I pursue as a purpose, I lose, inasmuch as the content of this purposiveness is true reality. Only finite, perishable things can be taken as purposes, not eternal being.

Thus purposive willing of the essential destroys it. Similarly, self-reflection destroys my being if by reflection I seek knowledge of it, and through knowledge possession and enjoyment of possession. "He who shows himself is not luminous. He who justifies himself is not prominent. He who boasts of himself is not given credit. He who brags does not endure for long" (24).

Purposiveness, self-reflection, self-striving, go hand in hand. The Tao is forsaken, the living action that flows from the Tao is impaired. Authentic life is destroyed.

The purposive man loses his encompassing awareness of opposites. He sees alternatives, always clinging to one as correct. In the world the Tao is manifested in antinomies, and a life rooted in the Tao embraces opposites. Thus to void opposites by purposive pursuit of one term, or to close one's eyes to them, is to fall away from the Tao. In order to take something as a purpose, I must differentiate. Thus the intentional man splits the organic pairs of opposites and isolates the terms. He ceases to see one in the other and to act accordingly; instead he sees one or the other, or vacillates between the two. This is to live on the surface of things and to lose the Tao. Instead of opening myself in devotion to the encompassing reality, I try to grasp reality in the form of a particular manifestation which I know.

B. *Nonaction* (wu wei) *as the source of ethics:* Purposive will, directed at finite particular things in the world, can gain fundamental reality only if it is gathered into a nonwilling. This nonwilling or nonaction is the core of Lao-tzu's ethos.

Wu wei is the spontaneity of the origin itself. It is not a doing nothing, not passivity, dullness of soul, a paralysis of the impulses. It is man's authentic action which he performs as though not acting. In this action the accent is not on works. It is all-embracing nonaction which encompasses all action, engenders it, and lends it meaning.

The antithesis between "action" and "nonaction" may suggest some sort of rule. But the origin to which this word refers cannot be subsumed under any law. It is not possible to give a rule for *wu wei* that would demand one thing and exclude another. For this would be to bring it back into the realm of purposive zeal, which precisely it transcends. What embraces the opposites cannot be adequately uttered in the oppositions of language. Thus Lao-tzu says of Tao: "Tao invariably takes no action, and yet there is nothing left undone" (37), and correspondingly he says of the Superior Man: "No action is undertaken, and yet nothing is left undone" (48). The nonaction of the Superior Man is an action of nonaction: "Therefore the sage manages affairs without action" (2).

If purposelessness denotes the activity that springs from the origin, purposiveness characterizes the activity that is born of particularizing, confining, intentional thinking. The former occurs unwilled and guides the purposive will; the latter is willed, but is ultimately without guidance and ground. Unintentionality starts from the Tao to arrive at being; intentionality starts from finiteness and arrives, by a process of destruction, at nothingness.

In unintentional action rooted in the Tao, a man does not demand assurance that he is acting well. He does not collect testimonials to his good will and try to prove himself in works. Unintentional action does not mean "Don't resist evil." For in Lao-tzu the accent is on the activity of a life grounded in Tao and one with it, not on suffering and sacrifice. Lao-tzu's nonaction is a living force out of the depths, while nonaction that "does not resist evil" becomes a weapon, a means of conquering by abandoning resistance, by shaming the enemy.

The collecting of testimonials to one's good actions and suffering in sacrifice are both highly intentional. Perhaps in no other philosophy is unintentionality, this concept so puzzling in its simplicity, taken so resolutely as the foundation of all ethical action. But this absence of all intentions cannot be defined, it cannot be invoked as a prescription. One can speak of it only indirectly.

c. Wu wei *and unison with the Tao:* It is as hard to characterize the Sage—the Saint, the Superior Man, the Perfect Man, etc.—as it is to speak of the Tao. Unison with Tao can never be taken as one of two opposites. Here there is no choice between two possibilities of equal rank. The description of the Saint is without clear contours; his reality conceals itself in oppositions. To put the accent on either of the two terms is to misunderstand it. For example:

"What is most perfect seems to be incomplete. . . . What is most full seems to be empty. . . . What is most straight seems to be crooked. The greatest skill seems to be clumsy. The greatest eloquence seems to stutter" (45).

"The Tao which is bright appears to be dark. . . . Great virtue appears like a valley (hollow). Great purity appears like disgrace. Far-reaching virtue appears as if insufficient. Solid virtue appears as if unsteady" (41).

We shall again encounter such antitheses in descriptions of the Sage. Taken literally, such statements are misleading, because they seem to press for rational decision between opposites or to play with paradoxical reversals. What they actually express is the very simple principle, which transcends all rational decisions by the gentle power of fulfilling certainty, the encompassing purposeless reality which guides us even in our purposive action.

Act through softness: "The weak and the tender overcome the hard and the strong" (36). "The softest things in the world overcome the hardest things in the world" (78). "The Way of the Sage is to act but not to compete" (81).

A metaphor is used to elucidate the strength of softness: "All things, the grass as well as trees, are tender and supple while alive. When dead they are

withered and dried. Therefore the stiff and the hard are companions of
death. The tender and the weak are companions of life. . . . The strong
and the great are inferior, while the tender and the weak are superior"
(76). Or: "The female always overcomes the male by tranquillity, and by
tranquillity she is underneath" (61).

Often weakness is likened to water. "There is nothing softer and weaker
than water, and yet there is nothing better for attacking hard and strong
things" (78). "The great rivers and seas are kings of all mountain streams
because they skillfully stay below them" (66). "Tao in the world may be
compared to rivers and streams running into the sea" (32). "The best is like
water. Water is good; it benefits all things and does not compete with them.
It dwells in places that all disdain" (8).

Selflessness: The Superior Man lives by the example of Tao: "Therefore
the Sage places himself in the background but finds himself in the fore-
ground. He puts himself away, and yet he always remains" (7). Thus there
are two selves, the desiring, self-seeking, self-reflecting self which seeks
riches and prestige, and the true self which comes to the fore only when
the other dies away. "He who conquers others is strong; he who conquers
himself is mighty" (33). This self-conquest has a number of consequences:

Freedom from desire: "The five colors cause one's eyes to be blind. The
five tones cause one's ears to be deaf. The five flavors cause one's palate to be
spoiled. Racing and hunting cause one's mind to be mad. Goods that are
hard to get injure one's activities. For this reason the Sage is concerned
with the belly and not the eyes" (12). "To force the growth of life means ill
omen. For the mind to employ the vital force means violence" (55). "It is
only those who do not seek after life that excel in making life valuable"
(75). "Only he who rids himself forever of desire can see the Secret Essences; he that has never rid himself of desire can see only the Outcomes"
(1). "When there are music and dainties, passing strangers will stay. But
the words uttered by Tao, how insipid and tasteless!" (35).

Freedom from vanity: "He does not show himself; therefore he is luminous. He does not justify himself, therefore he becomes prominent" (22).
"He accomplishes his task, but does not claim credit for it" (77).

Moderation: The Superior Man "manages affairs without action and
spreads doctrines without words" (2). Therefore (the Sage) "never strives
himself for the great, and thereby the great is achieved" (34).

"Withdraw as soon as your work is done" (9). The Sage "has no desire to
display his excellence" (77). "He accomplishes his task but does not
claim credit for it" (2). "He does not boast of himself; therefore he is given
credit" (22).

Knowledge: To live in unity with the Tao is at the same time to know
the Tao. To know it means also to live in it.

Knowledge of the Tao is not like a knowledge of something. Measured
by ordinary knowledge, knowledge of the Tao is as nothing: "The pur-

suit of learning is to increase day after day. The pursuit of Tao is to decrease day after day. It is to decrease and further decrease until one reaches
the point of taking no action" (48). "In penetrating the four quarters with
your intelligence, can you be without knowledge?" (10). "A wise man has
no extensive knowledge; he who has extensive knowledge is not a wise
man" (81).

Knowledge of Tao is not acquired from outside; it grows up within:
"One may know the world without going out of doors. One may see the
Way of Heaven without looking through the windows. The further one
goes, the less one knows" (47).

Knowledge of Tao is not a dispersed knowledge of many things; it is a
knowledge of the One: "To know eternity is to attain enlightenment" (55).
"He who does not know eternity runs blindly into disaster" (16).

All this means that the depth of Tao is disclosed only to the depth of
man. Tao withholds itself from man's surface thoughts and wrong thoughts,
from his desire and self-seeking, from his self-regard and acquisitiveness.
But in a man's depth rests the possibility of a knowledge that is one with
the source. If this depth is choked up, the waves of worldly life pass over it as
though it did not exist.

Consequently true self-knowledge is possible only with knowledge of the
Tao. "He who knows others is wise; he who knows himself is enlightened"
(33). This self-knowledge, which has nothing in common with self-reflection, with a desire to possess oneself by knowledge of oneself, is the knowledge of being oneself in Tao, which sees through and does away with the
false striving for selfhood. "To know that you do not know is the best. To
pretend to know when you do not know is a disease. Only when one
recognizes this disease as a disease can one be free from the disease. The
Sage is free from the disease. Because he recognizes this disease to be disease,
he is free from it" (71). Only the self-knowledge rooted in the primordial
source, the mother of all things, is positive: "When a man has found the
Mother, he will know the children accordingly; though he has known the
children, he still keeps to the Mother" (52).

Openness to all things: He who has regained Tao and thus extinguished
his self-striving and become himself lives amply. He sees things in their
fundamental being: "Knowing eternity, he is all-embracing. All-embracing,
he is without prejudice" (16). This comprehensiveness has far-reaching implications:

"The Sage has no fixed ideas. He regards the people's ideas as his own"
(49). There is no limit to his participation in the lives of others: "All things
arise, and he does not turn away from them" (2). He forsakes no man, for
"none is rejected" (27).

He is not afraid to treat all men alike: "I treat those who are good with
goodness. And I also treat those who are not good with goodness. . . . I am
honest to those who are honest, and I am also honest to those who are not

honest" (49). And he goes still further to demand of himself: "Repay hatred with virtue" (63).

But this breadth of scope also implies detachment. Perceiving and loving the essence, he sees through the finite appearance and becomes impervious to the particular. This indifference is not empty; it is filled with the Tao; imitating the Tao, he is beyond good and evil. He is not indifferent, but his profound vision of justice and love is concerned only with the essence: "Heaven and Earth are not humane; they regard all things as straw dogs. The Sage is not humane; he regards all people as straw dogs" (5).

The general attitude of the Sage: The Enlightened One behaves like the masters of antiquity: "Cautious, like one crossing a frozen stream in the winter, being at a loss, like one fearing danger on all sides, reserved, like one visiting. Supple and pliant, like ice about to melt. Genuine, like a piece of uncarved wood, open and broad, like a valley, merged and undifferentiated, like muddy water" (15). Or: he has "three treasures, guard and keep them: the first is deep love, the second is frugality, and the third is not to dare to be ahead of the world" (67). The Sage does not talk much. "Much talk will of course come to a dead end" (5).

The Sage is as simple and unself-conscious as a child: "He returns to the state of infancy" (28). "Can you be like an infant?" (10). "He who possesses virtue in abundance may be compared to an infant. . . . His bones are weak, his sinews tender, but his grasp is firm" (55).

The Sage is steadfast: ". . . it is impossible either to be intimate and close to him or to be distant and indifferent to him. It is impossible either to benefit him or to harm him. It is impossible either to honor him or to disgrace him" (56).

D. *The fall:* Lao-tzu's premise is that the world of men has fallen away from the Tao. Most men and consequently official opinion are far from the Tao. "Few in the world can understand the teaching without words and the advantage of taking no action" (43).

Why the fall? Antiquity possessed the Tao and lived in it (14, 15). The fall was brought about by men, but this event did not take the form of a natural catastrophe that happened once and for all in the past; rather, it happens every day. The fall is brought about by intentionality, self-reflection, and self-seeking.

According to Chuang-tzu, Lao-tzu stated the power and impotence of intentionality in his conversation with Confucius: "Finding the Tao is not a simple happening that can be willed; similarly losing the Tao is not a simple happening, but it can be willed." Which means: a man cannot come to the Tao by intentional willing. But finding Tao is not an automatic process; it is effected by the Tao within me and the Tao outside me. Nor does loss of the Tao take place of its own accord: it is brought about by a man's own action—"you can will it" by your intentionality and self-striving.

But whence comes this intentionality? Lao-tzu does not inquire. He does not ask whether the Tao might have remained one with world and man, whether the fall need not have taken place. For him the fall is a plain fact.

Stages in the fall: "He who follows the Tao becomes one with the Tao; he who follows virtue becomes one with virtue; he who follows corruption becomes one with corruption" (23). This means that intentional right conduct, or virtue, lies halfway between the Tao and corruption. Definite virtues and rules of conduct arise only when the Tao is forsaken. Indicative of a fallen state, they represent an attempt at partial salvation. Man has duties only after he has fallen away from the Tao. The seemingly noblest virtues are signs of a lower stage of humanity, which achieves authentic being only in unity with the Tao. "When the great Tao declined, the doctrine of humanity and righteousness arose. When knowledge and wisdom appeared, there emerged great hypocrisy. When the six family relationships are not in harmony, there will be the advocacy of filial piety and deep love to children. When a country is in disorder, there will be the praise of loyal ministers" (18).

Thus Lao-tzu develops a hierarchy descending from the lofty existence that moves in the Tao ("exalted virtue") to decreed virtue and the conventional respectability which ultimately uses force against those who do not comply with it: "The man of superior virtue takes no action, but has no ulterior motive to do so. The man of inferior virtue takes action, and has an ulterior motive to do so. The man of superior righteousness takes action, and has an ulterior motive to do so. The man of superior propriety takes action and when people do not respond to it, he will stretch his arms and force it on them. Therefore when Tao is lost, only then does the doctrine of virtue arise. When virtue is lost, only then does the doctrine of humanity arise. When humanity is lost, only then does the doctrine of righteousness arise" (38).

The hierarchy is also characterized from another point of view: "When the highest type of men hear Tao, they diligently practice it. When the average type of men hear Tao, they half believe in it. When the lowest type of men hear Tao, they laugh heartily at it" (41).

The way back to the Tao: No one is utterly rejected (27). In all men there is an inclination to esteem Tao voluntarily—without any command from outside (51). The essence is always unconsciously present even if it is consciously despised. The element of Tao that was instilled in creatures at birth is never wholly lost. Why should a man be rejected for his wickedness? "Why did the ancients highly value this Tao? Did they not say, 'Those who seek shall have it and those who sin shall be freed'?" (62).

Lao-tzu offers no instructions, no methods for finding the way back to the Tao, because unintentionality cannot be produced intentionally. He shows what is needful. But since this cannot be willed as a finite purpose, as a clearly knowable something, it is not possible to indicate a systematic method. Any method would be a perversion. Images and metaphors are not instructions.

Still, there is one apparent recipe: to follow the masters of antiquity: "Of old those who were the best masters were subtly mysterious and profoundly penetrating; too deep to comprehend. And because they cannot be comprehended, I can only describe them arbitrarily" (15).

However, there is an ambiguity in this turn back to ancient times. As Strauss says, it does not mean to repeat the past identically through knowledge of the literary tradition—that is the way of Confucius—it means to renew the eternal beginnings by retracing the threads of the Tao, which run through all history: "Hold on to the Tao of old in order to master the things of the present. From this one may know the primeval beginning (of the universe). This is called the bond of Tao" (14).

E. *Nothingness or eternity:* If asked what the meaning of life is, Lao-tzu would answer: To partake of Tao and so to be authentic, that is, eternal, immortal—to grasp the imperishable in the perishable. Lao-tzu expresses the idea of immortality with dark depth. "He who attains Tao is everlasting. Though his body may decay, he never perishes" (16). "He who may die but not perish has longevity" (33). "Use the light. Revert to enlightenment. And thereby avoid danger to one's life—this is called practicing the eternal" (52). "To control the vital breath with the mind means rigidity. (For) after things reach their prime, they begin to grow old, which means being contrary to Tao. Whatever is contrary to Tao will soon perish" (30).

Immortality here is an expression for participation in Tao, for rest in the timelessness of eternity, not an endless prolongation of existence either in another world or through a cycle of rebirths. The nature of immortality is never indicated in an image. Only the consciousness of eternity is elucidated. To life belongs death: "Man comes in to life and goes out to death" (50). But unchanging is what—when a man is at one with the Tao—relieves life and death of their danger, what remains when the body dies: "I have heard that one who is a good preserver of his life will not meet tigers or wild buffaloes, and in fighting will not try to escape from weapons of war. The wild buffalo cannot butt its horns against him, the tiger cannot fasten its claws in him, and weapons of war cannot thrust their blades into him. And for what reason? Because in him there is no room for death" (50). Here the "body" is taken metaphorically. Though his body may die, a man who is at one with Tao has no spot where death can strike. He is fearless because it no longer means anything to him to lose his body.

F. *The life of the follower of Tao—Lao-tzu—in the world:* In a world that has degenerated from a communion into a fabricated order of violence and law, a man who lives with true being will inevitably be reduced to solitude: not because he is an eccentric who shuns the world, but because society and government have lost their truth, that is, no longer follow the Tao; not because he is a maverick, but because the desires and pleasures, purposes and impulses of the crowd are far from Tao. Like Jeremiah and Heraclitus, Lao-tzu was one of the early solitary men, not because he wished to be, but by necessity.

In a few remarkable and very personal sentences Lao-tzu has described the life of the Sage in this world: "The multitude are merry, as though feasting on a day of sacrifice. Or like ascending a tower in the springtime. I alone am inert, showing no sign (of desires), like an infant that has not yet smiled. Wearied, indeed, I seem to be without a home. The multitude all possess more than enough. I alone seem to have lost all. Mine is indeed the mind of an ignorant man, indiscriminate and dull! Common folks are indeed brilliant; I alone seem to be in the dark. Common folks see differences and are clear-cut; I alone make no distinctions. I seem drifting as the sea; like the wind blowing about, seemingly without destination. The multitude all have a purpose; I alone seem to be stubborn and rustic. I alone differ from others, and value drawing sustenance from Mother (Tao)" (20).

In another passage Lao-tzu speaks of being misunderstood: "My doctrines are very easy to understand and very easy to practice, but none in the world can understand or practice them. My doctrines have a source; my deeds have a master. It is because people do not understand this that they do not understand me. Few people know me, and therefore I am highly valued. Therefore the Sage wears a coarse cloth on top and carries jade within his bosom" (70).

According to Ssŭ-ma Ch'ien, when the young Confucius came to see Lao-tzu, Lao-tzu condemned his projects for reform and said: "When the Sage finds his time, he rises; when he does not find his time, he lets the weeds pile up and goes. . . . Away with the master's weeds and with fanciful plans! All this is of no use to the master himself."

4. Tao and government

The truth—unison with the Tao—can be present in rulers, in governments, in the economic system, and even in warfare. Thus the truth of government resides in nonaction, in release, in imperceptible influence, in short, in weakness. The ruler is a single person. His character and conduct determine the life of the whole state. The sum of human affairs in the state will be what this one man is.

A. *The ruler:* The quality of rulers is shown by the way in which the people see them. "The best are those whose existence is (merely) known by the people. The next best are those who are loved and praised. The next are those who are feared. And the next are those who are despised. . . . They accomplish their task; they complete their work. Nevertheless their people say that they simply follow Nature" (17). "And the world will be at peace of its own accord" (37).

A perfect ruler "takes no action and therefore does not fail" (64). He acts by nonaction. "Can you love the people and govern the state without knowledge? (10). "Administer the empire by engaging in no activity" (57).

Accordingly a good ruler is humble, makes himself inconspicuous, demands nothing. "Therefore, in order to be the superior of the people, one must, in the use of words, place himself below them. And in order to be ahead of the people, one must, in one's own person, follow them. Therefore the Sage places himself above the people and they do not feel his weight. He places himself in front of them and the people do not harm him" (66). Such a ruler, who knows his rank but humbles himself and therefore calls himself "the Orphan," "the Lonely One," "the Destitute One" (39), "becomes the valley of the world" (28).

Only one who does not desire to govern can succeed in governing by nonactivity. If he is concerned with winning power and fears to lose it, he cannot truly govern. "They are difficult to rule because their ruler does too many things" (75). Elsewhere Lao-tzu speaks more severely of the bad ruler: "The courts are exceedingly splendid, while the fields are exceedingly weedy, and the granaries are exceedingly empty. Elegant clothes are worn, sharp weapons are carried, foods and drinks are enjoyed beyond limit, and wealth and treasures are accumulated in excess. This is robbery and extravagance" (53).

B. *The action of nonaction:* It is hard to understand this action by nonaction (*wu wei*) on the part of a ruler. It causes all beings to unfold, but truly and not arbitrarily: "If kings and barons can keep it, all things will transform spontaneously" (37).

It is a magical influence in keeping with Chinese universism: the ruler's harmony with Tao guides not only the kingdom but nature and all things upon the right course. It is the source of good harvests and prevents floods, drought, plagues, and wars. This magical conception is also to be found in Lao-tzu (if this passage is authentic and not a later addition): "If Tao is employed to rule the empire, spiritual beings will lose their supernatural power. Not that they lose their spiritual power, but their spiritual power can no longer harm people" (60). In Lao-tzu, however, this magical conception is secondary, though it is nowhere expressly disavowed.

The value of great models is often stressed. "Hold fast to the great form (Tao), and all the world will come" (35). "Virtue becomes deep and far-reaching, and with it all things return to their original state. Then complete harmony will be reached" (65). The influence of the Superior Man and consequently the imitation of the Tao put the realm and the people in order. By virtue of his inner being, man is the carrier of the model image. "The adherence of the empire is garnered by letting-alone" (57).

In the action of nonaction the essential is spontaneity. It would be absurd to suppose that we accomplish something by doing nothing. Nonaction is not a doing of nothing. It is the universal action which encompasses all plans, which precedes all definite action, which is neither passivity nor planless action. It is an intervention not according to mere finite ends, but rising from the source, the Tao itself. Any attempt to define the operation of this nonaction more closely would be out of place. Like the speculation that tries to penetrate into the Tao and the elucidation of individual nonaction, this political thinking is oriented toward the ineffable and undifferentiated.

Only at the next lowest step does differentiation set in—here definite discourse becomes possible. In negations: "The more taboos and prohibitions there are in the world, the poorer the people will be. The more sharp weapons the people have, the more troubled the state will be. . . . The more laws and ordinances are promulgated, the more thieves and robbers there will be" (57). Or the same statement is made in a positive but indefinite form: once intervention, prohibition, and command cease, all will become true and authentic "of its own accord." "I take no action and the people of themselves are transformed. I love tranquillity and the people of themselves become correct. I engage in no activity and the people of themselves become prosperous. I have no desires and the people of themselves become simple" (57). In contrast with this, only an external causality is expressed in the words: "The people starve, because the ruler eats too much tax-grain" (75).

Anyone who takes Lao-tzu's maxims as rules of conduct is bound to object: All that is impracticable, men are simply not made that way. But to raise such an argument is to forget that these are not rules for purposive action. Lao-tzu's maxims, which find their norm in not acting, not planning, not intervening, can only become meaningless if taken as a summons to act and to plan. Lao-tzu points the way to a possibility which is not a program for the understanding but, preceding all purposive political action, an appeal to the source within each man. Conceived as a concrete institution, realizable by finite means, his ideal would be a futile utopia of magical inactivity. But it is a truth insofar as it gives an intimation of the human possibility in political life. It may sound fantastic when Lao-tzu says: "If kings and barons would hold on to it, all things would submit to them spontaneously. Heaven and Earth unite to drip sweet dew. Without the command of men, it drips evenly over all" (32). But anyone who actively and by design introduced anarchy into the world on the supposition that men would automatically keep order because they are good, would merely be showing that he had misunderstood this philosophy. And even more so if he used force to quell the ensuing chaos. If the one who misunderstood Lao-tzu and introduced anarchy were a "saint," if he were sincere and consistent and men gave heed to him, he would still be doomed to destruction. Actually Lao-tzu had no intention of giving instructions by which to revolutionize human institutions. Keeping in mind his own maxim that no one knows how far he can go, he declares: "If one can overcome everything, then he will acquire a capacity the limit of which is beyond anyone's knowledge. When his capacity is beyond anyone's knowledge, he is fit to rule a state" (59).

c. *War and punishment:* How does Lao-tzu observe the ideal of nonaction in connection with the indispensable acts of political violence: in connection with war abroad and punishment at home? How is the principle "to act, not contend," manifested here?

War is in any case evil: "Fine weapons are instruments of evil, they are hated by men" (31). "Wherever armies are stationed, briers and thorns grow. Great wars are always followed by famines" (30). But there are situations in which even a Sage cannot avoid war. "When he uses them [weapons] unavoidably, he regards calm restraint as the best principle" (31). But once he makes up his mind, he imposes limits on his manner of fighting and conquering. "A good [general] achieves his purpose and stops, but dares not seek to dominate the world. He achieves his purpose but does not brag about it. . . . He achieves his purpose but only as an unavoidable step" (30).

Even in battle the principle of action by nonaction applies. Since "the weak and the tender overcome the hard and the strong" (36), since "the softest things in the world overcome the hardest things in the world" (43), Lao-tzu concludes with surprising consistency: "Therefore if the army is strong, it will not win. . . . The strong and the great are inferior, while the tender and the weak are superior" (76). "For deep love helps one to win in the case of attack, and to be firm in the case of defense" (67). Offensive warfare is expressly condemned. And even in battle one should act as little as possible: "A strategist of old has said: 'I dare not take the offensive but I take the defensive; I dare not advance an inch but I retreat a foot.' This means: 'To march without formation, to stretch one's arm without showing it, to confront enemies without seeming to meet them; to hold weapons without seeming to have them'" (69).

Lao-tzu describes the good warrior: "A skillful leader of troops is not oppressive with his military strength. A skillful fighter does not become angry. A skillful conqueror does not compete with people" (68). "Even when he is victorious, he does not regard it as praiseworthy. . . . For the slaughter of the multitude, let us weep with sorrow and grief. For a victory, let us observe the occasion with funeral ceremonies" (31).

The internal violence of the state is manifested in punishments, especially in the death penalty (72–74). Observance of the Tao is manifested in the judge's restraint. Only "what heaven hates" should be punished. But the heavenly judge is hidden. Hence the human judge who wishes to avoid unjust punishment derives comfort from the knowledge that an unjustly acquitted criminal will not evade punishment: "Heaven's net is indeed vast. Though its meshes are wide, it misses nothing" (73).

D. *Action in the changing world of things:* Men move away from the eternal Tao and return to it. It is essential to return each day afresh, but this does not mean to make the world over into something entirely new. For Lao-tzu and the Chinese there is no unique course of history, no undecided future, but only the eternal, infinitely agitated life of the Tao. In this life men fluctuate between harmony with Tao and deviation from it. Nonaction brings about perfect harmony.

Nonaction is not the repose of the onlooker but the dominant ground of action. Political life is fraught with unrest: enemies of the government, seeds of new enmity, changing conditions. Political nonaction is therefore attended by constant tension. While frantic activity never really accomplishes anything but imagines that by pursuing its aims it comes into possession of everything, everything is unchangingly present to him who acts on the ground of nonaction; he is alive to the immediate and remote consequences of every act: "People in their handling of affairs often fail when they are about to succeed. If one remains as careful at the end as he was at the beginning, there will be no failure" (64).

Thus the wise ruler lives in close contact with all things. He sees the beginnings, the seeds of development, and follows the maxim: "Prepare for the difficult while it is still easy. Deal with the big while it is still small" (63). All-important is the imperceptible touch at the right time. "What remains still is easy to hold. What is not yet manifest is easy to plan for. What is brittle is easy to crack. What is minute is easy to scatter. Deal with things before they appear. Put things in order before disorder arises. A tree as big as a man's embrace grows from a tiny shoot. A tower of nine stories begins with a heap of earth. The journey of a thousand *li* starts from where one stands" (64).

To make these imperceptible touches at all times, that is the difficult thing, for it means keeping in contact with the ground of things. That is why nonaction which produces universal order is far removed from light-heartedness. The nonactive ruler fastens himself to "the heavy." "Gravity is the root of lightness; stillness the master of agitation. Thus a nobleman travels all day without leaving his baggage-wagon. How then should a lord of ten thousand chariots conduct himself lightly in regard to his empire? If he conducts himself lightly, he will lose the root" (26).

E. *The desirable political condition:* In keeping with Chinese universism Lao-tzu sees human existence as a single hierarchically ordered realm extending from the one ruler through states, communities, and families to the individual man (54). This realm is not a planned institution, not an organization of functionaries such as that set up centuries later by Shih Huang-Ti, but a "spiritual thing." "He who acts on it harms it. He who holds on to it loses it" (29). Lao-tzu had before him the decaying feudal regime, whose original condition he regarded as in keeping with the Tao.

The general political condition was that of a number of small states connected by the one Empire. The best: "A small country with few people" (80). In order that life should be happy in this small state: "Let there be ten times and a hundred times as many utensils but let them not be used. . . . Even if there are ships and carriages, none will ride in them. Even if there are arrows and weapons, none will display them" (80). The relation between large and small states must be the right one: "A big state can take over a small state if it places itself below the small state. And the small state can take over a big state if it places itself below the big state" (61). Happy countries live quietly side by side; their people do not grow restless and enter into relations with one another: "Though neighboring communities overlook one another and the crowing of cocks and barking of dogs can be heard, yet the people there may grow old and die without ever visiting one another" (80).

F. *The truth of the primordial:* Idyllic descriptions of antiquity, injunctions to return to a precultural primitivism ("Where the people may be induced to return to the use of knotted cords" [namely, to the era before the invention of writing]) (80), may suggest that Lao-tzu's return to nature "was a return to barbarism." One more step, and this would indeed be so.

The statement that knowledge and enlightenment should be withheld from the people seems to point in the same direction. The wise ruler "constantly insures that the people are without knowledge and without desires and that those who have knowledge dare not act" (3). "In ancient times those who practiced Tao well did not seek to enlighten the people, but to make them ignorant. People are difficult to govern because they have too much knowledge. Therefore he who rules the state through knowledge is a robber of the state" (65). One step further, and this would be a devious method to make things easier for rulers by keeping the people in a state of ignorance.

Lao-tzu seems to condemn the lofty values of human culture and morality: "Abandon sageliness and discard wisdom; then the people will benefit a hundredfold. Abandon humanity and discard righteousness; then the people will return to filial piety and deep love. Abandon skill and discard profit; then there will be no thieves or robbers" (19). This is only a step from the indifferent quietism of a mere onlooker, who sees only his imaginings and rejects all visible reality.

We must try to consider such sentences in the light of the teachings as a whole and recognize the twofold meaning of the "primordial." The primary meaning, the meaning intended by Lao-tzu, is "that which is in keeping with the Tao." But it is remote, hidden, easy to mistake: one can gain an intimation of it, but not postulate it in terms of human reality. The second meaning is "what was in the beginning," the primitive, and this, because it is used as a metaphor for the first, is confused with it. Despite the power of his philosophical thought, despite his insight into the source of the highest human potentiality, Lao-tzu's sentences sometimes obscure and distort his original vision—and it is perfectly possible that the thinker himself was sometimes led astray.

II. CHARACTERIZATION AND CRITICISM

1. *The meaning of Lao-tzu*

A. *The contradiction: to speak of the ineffable:* "He who knows does not speak. He who speaks does not know" (56). Lao-tzu repeatedly utters this basic insight: The Sage "spreads doctrines without words" (2).

Thus Lao-tzu condemns his own attempt to communicate the deepest knowledge by way of what can be said. And indeed, every sentence that is spoken distracts from the fundamental truth. To take the statements literally is to tie oneself to objects. One must transcend both statement and object, that is, attain to the ineffable, in order to perceive the truth. Thus every statement must vanish in the ineffable if it is to become true.

Why, then, does Lao-tzu write a book? He offers no justification. It is only the legend which tells us that he did not wish to, that it was the frontier guard who demanded it, and that *nolens volens* Lao-tzu complied. We may answer: He meant these written statements to induce the reader to transcend them, he meant them to guide us, through reflection, to the ineffable. This work of Lao-tzu is the first great example of the indirect statement on which true philosophical thought always depends.

Only by communication does thought pass from man to man. Total silence can accomplish nothing. We are dependent on speaking and listening. In understanding itself and making itself understood by others, insight that is communicated must enter into the realm of the thought that reasons, names, defines, differentiates, and relates. Once it speaks, the ineffable philosophical insight comes into conflict with itself. But it is only in speech (and first of all in the discourse of the thinker with himself) that this insight becomes knowable to man.

B. *To what part of us is philosophical speech addressed?* Lao-tzu has told us: Not to the understanding, which is a knowledge of objects, not to the will, which aims at purposes and acts according to plans. Lao-tzu addresses the source within us, which is obscured by understanding and purposes. Hence he aims not at self-domination by the power of the will, but at a deeper examination of our impulses themselves.

What can thus be awakened lies dormant within us. Otherwise—though this Lao-tzu does not say—there is only an emptiness in which there is nothing to be awakened. He is confident that something, the Tao within us, can be awakened. But patience is needed to overcome resistance, obscurity, exhaustion, forgetfulness.

Lao-tzu's political discussion may serve as an example. His maxims come so close to rules that one is tempted to consider them as such and to think them through in this light. But then it becomes clear that in Lao-tzu all such rules are only metaphors. Taken as rules, they become false, for then they lead to passivity, while actually they are an expression for the ground of all activity. Properly understood, they arouse self-understanding, the reflection that flows from the all-embracing source. They combat the blind rage, thoughtless activity, and violence of those who see only the finite things about them.

These maxims can act as correctives to the tendency to regulate everything by laws and decrees. They can make us aware of the need to let things alone as much as possible. They can teach us to subordinate all laws and rules to a condition which itself cannot be formulated as a rule, but can only make itself heard in communication between man and man.

They convey ideas of the kind that we need if we are not to succumb to the endless activity which with all its purposiveness defeats its own purpose, so that everything turns out wrong in the end.

From time immemorial all states of any size have been administered by bureaucracies. It is striking to note that the vast majority of decisions in such bureaucracies have been made by purposive, "practical" men who, lacking a knowledge of the whole, produce the greatest absurdities with their purposiveness. The self-education of the active man and of the body politic requires reflection and responsibility to norms that go far beyond the mechanism of laws and prescriptions. Such responsibility demands an awareness of all regulations in the totality of life and of the relation between them. In all simplicity, it demands not only that we find the definite order appropriate to every situation, but also that all men be made freer in their daily lives, more available to the incalculable opportunities.

Lao-tzu's thoughts are addressed to the encompassing ground within us and outside us. They remind us of what is regularly forgotten in the realm of purposive will and finite understanding. Lao-tzu appeals to us in moments when, in daily life, in our work or political activity, our purposes have been divorced from that which must guide them if they are not to relapse into sterile futility, into a destructiveness that is only enhanced by activity and into perplexity in the face of the question: What for? Lao-tzu reminds us of what man must hold fast to if he is not to sink into the void.

c. *Lao-tzu's forms of thought:* Lao-tzu does not search; he knows the ground of being and speaks from the source. Filled with knowledge, he communicates. He answers without having been questioned.

He does not reflect on his methods of thought. But if we examine the ideas he communicates we note certain characteristic features.

1) Lao-tzu is a spur to our thinking, because his utterance is always incomplete, yet any attempt we may make to correct it proves inappropriate. For example: "If forced to give it a name, I shall call it Great. Now being great means functioning everywhere. Functioning everywhere means far-reaching. Being far-reaching means returning to the original point" (25). Strauss interprets: "If I force myself to give it a name, I call it great. But the absolutely great is the absolutely remote. It is this remote thing which pervades all things, which is now in my thinking, and therefore I designate it as returning."

2) The ideas with which the author endeavors to characterize the Tao end in antinomies, contradictions, paradoxes. Antinomies are joined together in various ways. They engender, complete, elucidate one another, they are relative to one another, follow or depend on one another. For example: "Being and nonbeing produce each other; difficult and easy complete each other; long and short contrast each other; high and low distinguish each other; sound and voice harmonize each other; front and behind accompany each other" (2). Another example: "The heavy is the root of the light. The tranquil is the ruler of the hasty" (26).

Lao-tzu uses these varied forms of antinomies in order to echo the ineffable, being through nonbeing, knowledge through nonknowledge, action through nonaction. Such repetition of an identical form may strike one as a tedious mannerism. In this game the antinomies hide, or extinguish one another, or change places: "Straight words seem to be their opposite" (78). We discern a dialectical form of thought, as yet unconscious of itself, the shifting of opposites into one another, the appearance of the one in the opposite of its other, the paradox of the unity of opposites. This is the form in which Lao-tzu speaks to us from the depths, summons us to meditation.

This playing with opposites disappoints us if we are looking for definite knowledge. It has compelling power only if it awakens a resonance in our own depths. Our finite understanding is supposed to be stood on its head as it were when it hears that the encompassing ground is nonbeing, from which springs being, nonknowledge, with which we apprehend the truth, nonaction whereby we act.

3) The Tao and what exists through the Tao can only be thought in

circular reasoning. It cannot be conceived as derived from something else or in relation to something else. Because it is unrelated to anything else, I can only express its being in the ground of nonbeing by saying that it is through itself; that it is known in nonknowledge by saying that it is known through itself; I can only express its action in nonaction by saying that it determines itself. This circular reasoning is an expression for the Tao's circling within itself. Thus: "Tao is a law unto itself" (25). I know it "through itself" (21); I know it "by itself" (54). If the veils are drawn aside and perversions done away with, if the will conforms to the Tao, the source is laid bare. And what awaits us there is not Nothingness but "itself."

The forms of progression, antinomy, reversal, and circular reasoning are means of bringing us closer to the source. This source is One. Hence Lao-tzu does not distinguish between metaphysics, ethics, and politics, as we have done in expounding his thought. Repeatedly Lao-tzu weaves them together in a few sentences. Consequently his thinking is always whole, whether he is speaking of politics, ethics, or metaphysics; that is to say, since in every case he is concerned with the common ground, he is always speaking of the same thing. When things are joined in the Tao, nothing is separate. When they are forsaken by the Tao, one separates from another and falsely sets itself up as the whole, as an absolute—the consequence is antinomies, intentionality, morality.

2. *Lao-tzu's successors*

Lao-tzu speaks from the standpoint of perfection or eternity. He speaks from the Encompassing to the Encompassing. If the objective content of his statements is taken literally as a knowable guide to action, its meaning is lost. In view of the form of Lao-tzu's communication it is easy to see how such misunderstanding could arise. What was meant metaphorically was taken as reality; what was meant as a guide for movements of thought was mistaken for the thought itself; what was meant as a way to the foundation of ethical life was interpreted as rule for intentional action. Lao-tzu spoke of the ineffable, an indispensable paradox of which he was well aware. But instead of being taken as a guide to the ineffable his words were misunderstood as objective knowledge of reality or as a prescription for ethical action or as a plan for proper government. Thus the imitation of Lao-tzu crystallized into certain set figures:

The hermit: Lao-tzu transcended the world with his thinking of the Tao, but he did not forsake the world, not even when he left his home. Drawing from his source in the Tao, he lived in the world itself. In thinking the Tao, he did not go the way of ecstasy; he did not seek access to the ground by modifications of consciousness, by inducing states of absence from the self and the world. In this sense, Lao-tzu was not a mystic. His thinking is a search for certainty in a movement that leads us to glimpse being in all things, confirms this vision, and makes possible its repetition. Lao-tzu saw and followed the Tao in the world. Hence metaphysics, ethics, and politics are aspects of his philosophy.

The profound peace of the Tao is present in every one of Lao-tzu's thoughts. This peace is beyond all aims and goals, it is the haven and refuge of all beings, it is source and shelter, end and perfection. But this peace is no passive peace of indifference, it is not vitalist contemplation of vegetative existence, but rest amid the unrest of suffering at the hands of a world alien to the Tao. It is present even in the suffering of loneliness, in the necessity to live like a fool in a world that has become a stranger to the Tao.

In the following misunderstandings, the meaning of Lao-tzu is diametrically reversed: Freedom from desire, said Lao-tzu, is the condition of vision of the Tao. From a distortion of this idea it is inferred that a man without passions or a man who does nothing comes closer to the source. Lao-tzu suffered, but he did not hide away from the world or deny its existence. In a distortion of his thinking, the world was absolutely rejected for its corruption. Hermits and monks took up his maxims in disregard of their meaning. From time immemorial China had known its hermits, who broke with family, community, and state, to live alone in the wilderness. Solitude is praised in the ancient songs of the *Shih Ching:* "Solitude by brook and rivulet is the serene choice of the Saint. He is alone in his sleeping, his waking and his speaking . . . solitude on the mountain slope . . . Solitude on the lofty summit . . ." There have been monks at all times in China. Chinese monasticism was exclusively Taoist until the advent of Buddhism. The Taoist monks invoked the name of Lao-tzu.

The "Epicurean": Conversely, the repose of the Tao could also be found in the world. Then the Tao was interpreted as a refined art of spiritual enjoyment of life under all conditions. Real life is not taken as a task, as a set of duties to be performed in family, profession, and state. The individual achieves a happy and peaceful life by adapting himself to all sorts of realities which are not to be taken seriously in themselves. This achieving of the beautiful life is developed into a high art. One is reminded of the old story about the three vinegar drinkers. Vinegar is the symbol of life. Confucius finds it sour, Buddha bitter, Lao-tzu sweet. Down through the centuries the Confucians have attacked Lao-tzu, whom they identify with an artificial discipline of living. Chu Hsi (1131–1200) declared that Lao-tzu, whether speaking of emptiness, purity, nonaction, or self-abasement, thought only of his own advantage, that he came into conflict with no one and always went about with a satisfied smile.

The man of letters: Chuang-tzu was the most famous of Lao-tzu's disciples. Unlike the *Tao Tê Ching,* he is easy to read even in translation, witty, exciting, imaginative, rich in fluent disquisitions and sharp aphorisms, skillful in modulating his ideas and in varying his forms. An inventive writer, he holds our attention by anecdotes, conversations, situations.

But he is a far cry from Lao-tzu. Lao-tzu moves us by his fundamental earnestness, by his freedom from vanity, as much by the truth and depth of his suffering as by his serenity. Chuang-tzu startles us with surprise effects; his prevailing mood is one of irony and skepticism; he treats Lao-tzu's ideas as material for his literary invention. One feels that he deliberately set out to produce literature. Thus the meaning of every single word of Lao-tzu is transformed. What in Lao-tzu was painful paradox, indispensable detour in the quest for the unattainable, and as such so profoundly appealing, becomes the literary method and artistic life of the Sage. Thus Lao-tzu can be reached only by long reflection and is inexhaustible. Chuang-tzu seems easily understandable, but what ought to have been the substance of any imitation of Lao-tzu is lost.

The atmosphere in Lao-tzu is peaceful; in Chuang-tzu it is polemical, full of arrogance, mockery, contempt. Chuang-tzu seems to know nothing of what Lao-tzu discloses as the strength of weakness, as the gentle power of the lowly, as the force of the water that flows always downward to the most lowly places; he knows nothing of Lao-tzu's humility. Lao-tzu bears the immeasurable suffering of the world's estrangement from the Tao. Chuang-tzu expresses only man's natural grief over transience and death, his plaint over the vain question: Whence, whither, and to what end?

Chuang-tzu's admirable gift of invention, his penetrating ideas about world and reality, about language, his insight into psychological states, his richness, make him one of the most interesting Chinese authors. But he must not be confused with Lao-tzu, in relation to whom he is not even an adequate commentator.

The magician: Lao-tzu was invoked by Taoists who (like mystics throughout the world) strove by breathing techniques to induce states of profound revelation; he was invoked by those who strove to find or make the elixir, the potion, of immortality, by magicians who claimed to walk on clouds, to be present at any place they wished whenever they wished.

The power politician: The maxims concerning the Tao and the Superior Man who is beyond good and evil were divested of their meaning and twisted into a system for conducting human affairs without recourse to norms or morality. Insurrectionists perverted the ideal of eternal anarchic peace in a life according to the Tao into a justification of their efforts to induce such a state of affairs by violence. A Confucian said critically that Lao-tzu looked upon men as clay figures, that his heart remained cold, that even when a man was killed he felt no pity, and that this was why his supporters often lent themselves to rebellion and betrayal.

Ch'in Shih Huang-Ti, the greatest of Chinese tyrants, who in the third century B.C. reorganized the Chinese Empire along unprecedented totalitarian lines based on technical planning, had the Confucian books burned but preserved the Taoist scriptures along with works on military, agricul-

tural, and other useful subjects. He desired individual immortality and
sent an expedition to the islands of the eastern sea, where the potion of
immortality was to be found. It is worth remembering that this ruler was
a Taoist. It is the profoundest thinker who can be the most radically perverted.

3. *Lao-tzu's historical position and limitations*

Lao-tzu is rooted in an immemorial anonymous tradition. His achievement
was to give the mythological world view new depth and to transcend it in
philosophical thought. The original form of this thinking is associated with
his name. He was followed not only by an elegant literature which made
his thought more accessible, but also by superstition; his maxims were distorted into tangible prescriptions. But down through the ages he has remained an awakener of true philosophy.

Historically, Lao-tzu's greatness is inseparable from the Chinese spirit.
His limits are its limits: his mood is one of serenity amid suffering. He
knows neither the threat of Buddhist rebirths, and hence the urge to depart
from this wheel of torment, nor the Christian Cross, the dread of inexorable
sin, man's dependence on the grace of redemption by the sacrificial death
of the incarnate God. One might be tempted to say that the Western and
Indian conceptions are hideous nightmares measured by the naturalness of
the Chinese and regard the early Chinese as fortunate for having escaped
such phantasms. But this absence of the historical intuitions of Indian and
Western mankind is more than an absence of the unnatural and absurd.
What charm is exercised by this Chinese spirit, which could lament so
grievously, but did not rebel against the ground of all things or succumb
to abject obedience to the unfathomable in the shape of revealed authority.
And yet there was something lacking. It is this deficiency that makes
Chinese thought, for all its charm, seem so alien to us, as though here the
abyss of horror had never opened in all its depth. The Chinese never developed an art of tragedy, and great as their vision and experience of evil
have been, the tragic has remained inaccessible to them.

How then do we perceive this deficiency, this limit in Lao-tzu? Like all
the great philosophers of mankind, Lao-tzu thinks from out of the Encompassing and does not allow himself to be fettered to any content of
knowledge. His all-embracing thinking omits nothing. He himself cannot
be identified as a mystic, a moralist, a political thinker. His profound peace
in the Tao is gained in a transcending of all finiteness, but in his thinking
finite things themselves, insofar as they are true and real, are permeated by
the Tao. The limit of such philosophizing is first disclosed by what is or
is not represented as in need of being transcended, by the links which are
indispensable to our temporal consciousness. For these links are the stages

of transcending, or the modes of the actuality of the real, through which the ground is first experienced. They are preserved in transcending and give the transcending, which without them would be empty, its content. The limits perceptible to us in Lao-tzu are not in the summit of his philosophizing, but in the intermediate stages.

The fundamental intuition in which all these intermediate stages are situated can perhaps be schematized as follows: For the Chinese mind the world is natural process, living cycle, the tranquilly moving cosmos. All deviations from the Tao of the whole are incidental and temporary; they are always reabsorbed into the imperishable Tao itself. To us Westerners the world is not a self-contained whole; it is related to something that cannot be understood on the basis of the world as natural process. The world and our mind are engaged in the tension of struggle, with each other and with the other-worldly; they are a decisive event in the struggle, they have a unique historical meaning. Lao-tzu does not know the symbol of the angry, demanding God, the God who battles and desires battle.

In the world, in time, in finiteness—in the area of the intermediate stages —we need what is lacking in Lao-tzu: life in question and answer and new question, the weight of the alternative, of decision and resolution, the fundamental, paradoxical truth that the eternal is decided in time. In Lao-tzu there is not so much as a suggestion of this boundless self-reflection, of this movement which (in contrast to perfect peace in the Tao) never ceases in time; he lacks this self-clarification, this dialogue with oneself, this eternal process of dispelling the self-deceptions and mystifications and distortions which never cease to beset us.

NAGARJUNA

Roughly from the first to the eighth century A.D. a philosophy based on logical operations grew up in India, both among the Hindus (the Nyaya school) and among the sects of Mahayana Buddhism. The most famous of the Buddhist thinkers were Nagarjuna (roughly second century A.D.), Asanga, Vasubandhu, Dignaga, Dharmakirti (seventh century). The literature has come down to us not in its original form but in later works, which became the fundamental texts of philosophical Buddhism, especially in China.

In this world of dialectical logic as the conscious expression of a way of life, the Shunyavadin, the sect to which Nagarjuna belonged, drew the most radical conclusions from the assumptions common to all Buddhist sects. All is empty, they taught. Things have only a momentary, phantom existence without permanent substance. Consequently true knowledge lies in Emptiness. I acquire it by detachment, that is, by a thinking that is free from signs and signification, stirred by no inclination or goal. This doctrine is called the "diamond-splitting Perfection of Wisdom"; it also calls itself the middle way (*madhyamika*) between the two theses that life is and that life is not: emptiness (*shunya vada*) has neither being nor nonbeing. Perfect Wisdom lies in perfect freedom from conflict.

We gain an idea of this philosophy from two books, *Prajñāpāramitā* and *Nagarjuna*. They have been translated from Chinese and Tibetan; the Sanskrit originals have been lost. Along with these works we must also consider a few passages in the *Sutra of the Forty-two Chapters*. We can gain little idea of Nagarjuna as an individual. We know him only as a representative of this extreme possibility of transcending metaphysics by means of metaphysics.

I. THE OPERATIONS OF THOUGHT

1. *A fundamental concept* in this thinking is *dharma*. All existence is *dharma*. *Dharma* is thing, attribute, state; it is content and consciousness of content; it is subject and object, order, creation, law, and doctrine. The underlying

conception is "that the content of the world is not an established order or form, but a process of ordering and form-giving, and that every order must make way for another order, every form for another form" (Oldenberg). Although each *dharma* is independent, the *dharmas* are listed, some seventy-five of them, to form a system of categories. *Dharma* has as many meanings as our Occidental "Being." The word cannot be translated, because its meanings are all-embracing.

2. *The goal* of this thinking is stated to be *"nonattachment"* to the *dharmas*. By not accepting them, not apprehending them, by breaking free from them, I attain Perfect Wisdom. Consequently the Enlightened One (Bodhisattva) "will stand outside appearance, outside sensation, outside concepts, outside forms, and outside consciousness" (*Pr.* 37).

Children and common men cling to the *dharmas*. Though the *dharmas* are not real, they form images of them. After imagining them, men cling to name and form. Not so the Enlightened One: in learning, a Bodhisattva does not learn any *dharma*. "To him the *dharmas* are present in a different way."

Detachment requires a last step. I might suppose that at least the doctrine exists, that this one *dharma* has being, that the Buddha existed, that the Bodhisattvas who attain Perfection of Wisdom exist. Are they not reality? No, this too is empty. "I do not see that *dharma* Bodhisattva, nor a *dharma* called Perfect Wisdom" (35–53). Perfection of Wisdom cannot be perceived, it is not present as an existing thing. For we cannot speak of appearance in the face of that which is nonperception of appearance, nor speak of consciousness where there is no awareness of sensation, concept, form. This is the fundamental and radical idea: to detach myself from all things and then from detachment; to cling to nothing.

3. The *instrument* of this thinking is the dialectic as it had been developed by Indian logic. Such dialectic alone enables me to understand and achieve complete detachment. It breaks down every concept, undermining its application to an object. These operations, in which Nagarjuna was particularly ingenious, became in their turn a kind of doctrine. Let us carry out a few of them:

a) *All designations are meaningless:* When I speak, I suppose that the signs (*nimitta*) I employ "signify" things. If for example I wish to speak of becoming and perishing, I must devise different signs. But designation and differentiation lead us into error. Designation and thing designated cannot be one, nor can they be different. For if they were one, the word would burn when we said "fire." If they were different, there could be no designation without a thing designated, and conversely no thing designated without a designation; hence they cannot be different. Thus designation and thing designated are neither the same nor different; thus in my discourse they are nothing at all. But if the designation is said to be a mirror image, as a mere image it is again false. Thus what is thought and differentiated under a false designation cannot truly exist.

Since designation and thing designated can be neither one nor different, distinctions between things designated—such as coming and going, becoming and perishing—are also untenable. To live by signs is to live in illusion, far from Perfect Wisdom. But every man lives by signs when he lives in the realm of appearance—whether he assumes that "appearance is a sign," or that "appearance is empty," when he lives in the assumption "I live" or "I am conscious."

With the resources of language there is no escape from speech through significations (signs). Every sentence ensnares me anew in what I was trying to escape from.

b) *To judge by the evidence, everything is and at the same time is not*: All statements can be proved or refuted by reference to evidence. As an instance: "Perishing" is untenable, for in the world things are seen to be imperishable, for example: the rice exists today because it has always existed. Since it is present, there is no "perishing." "Becoming" is also untenable: in the world all things are seen to be "unproduced." And in the same vein: Destruction is not, for the rice plant sprouts from the seed. Since becoming is perceived, there is no destruction. Or the other way around: There is no eternity, because eternal things do not occur in the world: at sprouting time the rice seed is not seen. Thus one thing after another is demonstrated by evidence: things are not one, they are not different; there is no coming, there is no going, etc.

This notion is based on the fact that all categories can be found somewhere in the world. Instead of asking where certain categories apply and where they do not apply, the author shows that they are always applicable in certain respects; then he goes on to endow them with absolute validity, and once they are taken as absolutely valid, he easily disproves them.

c) *How being and nonbeing are refuted*: Being is, nothing is not. This position, as well as the contention that nothing exists, is rejected by Nagarjuna. He takes the following steps, each time setting up a thesis and refuting it to make way for a new thesis which is refuted in turn.

1): *Things exist independently*. No, for to exist independently means to have come into being without causes and conditions. All things owe their existence to causes and conditions. Consequently nothing exists independently, everything exists through something else.

2): *If there is no independent existence, then at least there is otherness*. No, for if there is no independent existence, what would be the source of otherness? It is an error to call the independent existence of another thing otherness. If there is no independent being, there is also no otherness.

3): *Even without independent being and otherness, there must be things*. This is impossible. For what being can there be without being-as-such and being-different? Consequently: Only where there are being-as-such and being-different, is being attained.

4): *Then there is nonbeing*. Not at all. For without being there can be no nonbeing. What people call nonbeing is only the otherness of a being.

The core of the idea is the demonstration that both being and nonbeing are equally impossible.

If there were being-as-such (independent being), its nonbeing would not be. Never can something that is in itself become other. If there really exists something that is in itself, otherness is not possible. But if there is no being-as-such, in relation to what can there be otherness or nonbeing? It follows that both being and nonbeing are untenable. Thus the follower of Perfect Wisdom must take neither being nor nonbeing as his foundation, he must assert neither that the world is eternal nor that it is perishable.

Those who see being-as-such and being-otherwise, being and nonbeing, have failed to understand the teachings of the Buddha. When the Buddha refutes being, men infer falsely that he asserts nonbeing. When the Buddha refutes nonbeing, it is falsely inferred that he asserts being. Actually, he refuted them both, and both views must be abandoned.

d): *The technique of refutation* consists in methodically demonstrating that every possible statement can and must be refuted: "The Sankhyas assume that cause and effect are one; thus, to refute them, assert: they are not one. The Vaisesikas assume that cause and effect are different; thus to refute them, assert: they are not different."

This method crystallized into a typical formula, which consisted in considering four possibilities one at a time and in rejecting them all: 1. Something is. 2. It is not. 3. It both is and is not. 4. It neither is nor is not. Thus every possibility of a final valid statement is excluded.

The consequence is that everything can be formulated negatively and positively. The Buddha taught one thing and the opposite as well. Not only is the opposition between true and false transcended but also the opposite of this opposition. In the end no definite statement is possible. The four statements are repeated and rejected in connection with each *dharma*. For example: There is an end; there is no end; there is and is not an end; the end neither is nor is not. Or: After Nirvana the Buddha exists; he does not exist; he exists and does not exist; he neither exists nor does not exist.

e): *What is refuted:* The operation is constantly repeated, but the content varies—modes of thought, opinions, statements, in short, the categories of Indian philosophy, are refuted in turn. Just as the nature of a flame depends on the kind of fuel consumed, so the operation of refutation depends on what is refuted. Many of these categories are familiar to us, others are not; but it must not be forgotten that translation obscures the specifically Indian coloration of such concepts as being and nonbeing, becoming and perishing, causality, time, matter, self, etc.

Summary of the Doctrine

a) There are two truths: the veiled worldly truth and the highest truth. According to the veiled truth, all the *dharmas* have a cause. According to the highest truth, they are perceived to be without cause. But the highest truth cannot be obtained independently of the veiled truth. And Nirvana is not obtained without the highest truth. Thus the Buddha's doctrine is dependent on two truths, or in other words, the true can be attained only through the false. But this path can be traveled only with the help of enlightenment, which comes to me from the highest truth. Thanks to this enlightenment, I cease, even in my thinking of the inherently empty *dharmas,* to accept the illusion of the world; even while I think the *dharmas* and participate in them, I cease to cling to them.

b) Thus the one is conceived in terms of two truths. But this conception leads to two opposed views: all things do and do not possess independent being. If things exist independently and as such, they are without cause and condition. Then there is no cause and no effect, no action and no agent, no becoming and no perishing. If things are held to be nonexistent, all becomes phantasm. Nagarjuna rejects both these views in favor of "Emptiness." Things do not exist eternally in themselves, but at the same time they are not nothing. They are midway between being and nonbeing, but they are empty. There is no *dharma* that has come into being independently, hence all *dharmas* are empty.

Nagarjuna calls this the doctrine of "conditioned becoming." For him it is an expression of the deepest truth. But in formulating it, he is compelled to employ terms that are inadequate from the standpoint of his own method, as when he sums up the doctrine: "Without becoming, also without perishing, not eternal, also not cut-off, not one, also not differentiated, without coming, also without going—who can thus teach conditioned becoming, the quiet extinction of development: before him I bow my head."

This view of the emptiness of things in "conditioned becoming" saves the reality of the conquest of suffering, the reality of the way. For if there were independent being, there would be no coming-into-being and no passing-away. What exists through itself, cannot come into being and will endure forever. Thus if there is independent being, nothing further can be attained, nothing more can be done, because everything already exists. If there were independent being, living creatures would be free of diversity. There would be no suffering. But if things are empty, there is becoming and perishing, action and accomplishment. To contest the emptiness of things is to contest their actuality in the world. Suffering is a reality precisely because it does not exist in itself and is not eternal.

c) This has an amazing consequence, which is clearly formulated: If nothing authentically is, must we not infer the nonexistence of the Buddha, of the doctrine, of knowledge, of ritual practice, of the congregation, of monks, of the Sages who have attained the goal? The answer is that they do exist in emptiness, which is neither being nor nonbeing. Because there is emptiness, the Buddha exists. If things were not empty, if there were no becoming, no perishing, and no suffering, there would be no Buddha; nor would there be his doctrine of suffering, the negation of suffering, and the way to the negation of suffering. If suffering existed independently, it could not be destroyed. If the way existed in itself, it would not be possible to travel it, for eternal being precludes motion and development. If we postulate independent being, there is nothing more to be achieved. Hence the Buddha, his teaching, and what is achieved by his teaching are all in emptiness. Only when a man sees all the *dharmas* as conditioned becoming in emptiness, can he see the doctrine of the Buddha, the Four Noble Truths, and transcend suffering.

Those who take the Buddha's doctrine of unsubstantiality as an argument against that same doctrine, have not understood it. Their argument ceases to apply if all thought, representation, and being are seen in emptiness.

Those who accept emptiness accept everything, the worldly and the transcendent. To those who do not accept emptiness, nothing is acceptable.

Those who differentiate the four views of the logical schema move in veiled truth. They are beset by many kinds of representations. They still cling to the alternative: "If this is true, the other is false." But for those in whom the eye of Perfect Wisdom has opened, the four views disappear.

The spiritual eye of those who suppose that they see the Buddha through developments such as: being—nonbeing, eternal—not eternal, body—spirit, etc., has been injured by these developments. They no more see the Buddha than a man born blind sees the sun. But those who see conditioned becoming, see suffering, its coming-into-being and the manner of its annihilation, that is, they see the way, just as a man endowed with eyes is enabled by the shining of a light to see the appearances of things.

II. THE MEANING OF THE DOCTRINE

1. Teachability: Insofar as this method of refuting every assertion of being or nonbeing is represented as universally valid, we have before us a doctrine. As such it has been called negativism or nihilism. But this is not correct. For what this doctrine seeks is an authentic truth which cannot itself become a doctrine. Hence, all its operations end in paradoxical statements that cancel each other out and so point to something else: "The Buddha says: My doctrine is to think the thought that is unthinkable, to practise the deed that is not-doing, to speak the speech that is inexpressible, and to be trained in the discipline that is beyond discipline" (*The Sutra of the Forty-two Chapters*, 18).

Actually, the doctrine was set forth as a doctrine, both orally and in writing, and was also reflected in exercises and in ethical practice. "A Bodhisattva must above all hear this Perfection of Wisdom, take it up, bear it in mind, recite, study, spread, demonstrate, explain and write it" (*Pr.* 36–38). But this is only the first stage. Hearing the doctrine, the monk who is not yet at the goal "follows his trust" (*Pr.* 38). He is not yet in the truth. The truth is not arrived at by any knowable, logically determined content, but "awakens suddenly to unexcelled perfect enlightenment" (*Pr.* 41).

This process of hearing and learning until the truth itself is kindled is a process of thought which seizes upon the whole man. The operations as such leave nothing in place, they confuse the mind and make it dizzy. Accordingly: "If, hearing these thoughts, he is not alarmed and does not take fright . . . , if in the presence of such a doctrine he does not sink down in terror, if the backbone of his mind is not broken . . . then this man should be instructed in the Perfection of Wisdom" (*Pr.* 35, 77).

Reading the texts, we see that the doctrine consists in practice, in constant repetition, and that this repetition with variations creates a mood of its own which is in keeping with the content of the doctrine. The logical element itself is seldom clearly and systematically developed. The dialectic takes the form of mere lists. This is perhaps appropriate to the mode of thought. For this negative logic prepares the way, not for a positive insight developed in logical terms, but for a silence filled from another source. Here all reasoning annuls itself.

This is illustrated by a number of anecdotes (related after Hackmann). Bodhidharma asked his disciples why they did not express their experience. All the answers are correct, but each in succession comes closer to the authentic truth. The first disciple says that the experience is unrelated to spoken words, though associated with them in instruction. The second: The experience is like a paradise, but vanishes immediately and therefore cannot be expressed. The third: Since all existing things have only an illusory existence, the content of his experience, once framed in words, would be mere illusion and emptiness. The fourth, instead of answering, steps before the master in an attitude of veneration, and keeps silence. The last has given the truest answer and becomes the patriarch's successor.—Or: Bodhidharma speaks with the Emperor Liang Wu Ti. The Emperor says: I have never ceased to build temples, to commission the writing of sacred books, to give new monks permission to enter monasteries. What is my merit?—None at all. All this is only the shadow that follows the object and is without true being.—The Emperor: What then is true merit?—To be surrounded by emptiness and stillness, immersed in thought. Such merit cannot be gained by worldly means.—The Emperor: What is the most important of the holy doctrines?—In a world that is utterly empty, nothing can be called holy.—The Emperor: Who is it who confronts me thus?—I do not know.

But now the question arises: Not finding, not perceiving, not seeing a Perfection of Wisdom, what Perfection of Wisdom should I teach? Answer: Practice in such a way that in exercising you do not pride yourself on the idea of illumination. This thought is pure, for it is in fact nonthought. But because this thought of Perfect Wisdom is nonthought, is it therefore nonexistent? The answer: In a nonthought there is neither being nor nonbeing; hence it is impossible to ask whether the thought that is nonthought exists (*Pr.* 35).

2. *The purpose of the operations:* This thinking demands that we should never hold fast to a position but free ourselves from all assertions, that we should not rely on any *dharma,* neither on sound nor tangible things nor thoughts nor representations, that we should shatter all explanations, for "what is explained is precisely not explained" (*Pr.* 149). Consequently, we should admit no alternative thinking, no decision between opposites, but let all differentiations cancel themselves out. There is no limit, no ultimate point of rest, but only, through the failure of thought, a transcending of thought into a more-than-thought, into the Perfection of Wisdom. The emptiness that is arrived at by compelling thought will awaken the infinite meaning of the unthinkable.

Thus thinking becomes a perpetual overturning of thoughts. Every statement as such is absurd. All statement is self-negating. But this self-negation can kindle the truth. The authentic truth can become manifest only by negating itself in statement. Thus the way leads through a truth which when thought is no truth, to the truth which is manifested in ceasing to be thought. This authentic truth is a thinking that lives by the combustion of provisional truth.

But what is this nonthought attained by thought, this liberation from all liberations? The answer: Apprehending that which cannot be apprehended, it is itself not apprehended, for it can no longer be apprehended by signs (*Pr.* 38). When he has arrived at that point, the Bodhisattva "stands fast in the sense of not-standing" (*Pr.* 48); "he will not stand somewhere; in Perfect Wisdom he will stand in the mode of not-standing."

The teacher of this doctrine contradicts himself whenever he speaks, and such self-contradiction becomes a deliberate method. Questioned from the standpoint of any *dharma* whatsoever, he can always find a way out. Because he is independent of all the *dharmas* he does not, in speaking, come into contradiction with the essence of his doctrine, although he does contradict all statements, even his own. Consequently, every false statement is justified, because statement as such is always false.

This thinking may be interpreted as follows: Through thinking man has become fettered to the thought content, the *dharmas;* this is the reason for our fall into the suffering of existence. Through the same thinking, but in the opposite direction, the thought content is dissolved. Fettered by thought, we employ the weapons of thought to destroy its fetters and so penetrate to the freedom of nonthought.

Nagarjuna strives to think the unthinkable and to say the ineffable. He knows this and tries to unsay what he has said. Consequently he moves in self-negating operations of thought. The obvious logical flaws in the texts are only in part mistakes that can be corrected; for the rest, they are logically necessary, resulting from an attempt to do the impossible—namely, to express absolute truth.

In Nagarjuna's thinking we may find a formal analogy on the one hand to the dialectics of the second part of Plato's *Parmenides,* and on the other hand to modern symbolic logic (Wittgenstein). Symbolic logic might be employed as a means of systematically correcting the mistakes which, in the Indian texts as in the far more highly developed thinking of Plato's *Parmenides,* are so disturbing to modern Occidentals. Only occasionally does the logical operation effected in the Indian texts break through the mists in full clarity. But on the other hand, these Indian philosophers, as well as Plato, raise the question: What is the meaning of these purely logical endeavors? Only in Wittgenstein do I find an inkling of what it might mean to carry thought, by pure thought free from error, to the limit where it shatters. Amid the clarity which is possible today, but which as mere clarity remains an empty pastime, the depth that is discernible in the Indian texts for all their cloudiness might well become a spur to self-reflection.

3. The uses of logic: To the analytic mind which thinks in terms of alternatives, such concepts as motion, time, the One are unthinkable. In the Western world the search for logical operations with which these problems, always under specific assumptions, can in some measure be mastered, has opened up magnificent fields of finite knowledge, in which even the infinite, in certain forms or under certain aspects, has become an instrument of finite thinking.

In India the barest beginnings were made toward the consideration of these problems. These beginnings served an entirely different purpose from the solution of specific problems (a purpose which might, in view of the subtle logical insights of recent centuries, be revived in a sense which today cannot be foreseen).

Operations which shatter all definite statements, so that everything dissolves into otherness, opposition, contradiction, so that all determinations vanish and no position stands fast, must ultimately lead either to nothingness or to an intimation of authentic being, even if it can no longer be called being. Or to put it in another way: The end is either a playful concern with "problems" or a state of mind which in such methods finds a means of understanding and actualizing the self, an attitude of perfect superiority to the world, of perfect detachment from all things and from one's own existence, and hence of perfect superiority to oneself.

In Asia the visible embodiment of this way of thinking may be a monastic life of meditation enhanced by practice, or it may take the form of rites and cults, magic and gestures. But the dialectic of the philosophers served neither the one nor the other. Within these embodiments, its aim was negative: the rejection of all metaphysics as a knowledge of another, objective being distinct from myself (as in the Hindu system); and positive: the acquisition of Perfect Wisdom which may be termed nonthought, because through thought it has become more-than-thought.

4. Against metaphysics: Nagarjuna rejects all metaphysical thinking. He rejects the creation of the world, whether by a God (Isvara) or by purusha, whether by time or by itself. He opposes attachment to all fixed concepts—of attributes, being as such, atoms, etc.; he opposes the view that everything will be destroyed and the view that everything is eternal; he rejects the notion of the self.

The metaphysics he has rejected is replaced by this logical thinking. Buddha's fundamental attitude, the rejection of ontological questions in favor of salvation and the truth necessary for this salvation, is carried to its logical conclusion. The earlier ontological speculation becomes a clarification through movements of thought which cancel each other out.

Over a period of centuries Indian philosophy had elaborated a rich logic. But this logic had been intended for public discussion and worldly science. Even in later centuries certain Tibetan sects looked upon logic as a worldly discipline (Stcherbatsky). But here logic became a means of union with authentic being, not through ontological knowledge but through a process which consists in the self-combustion of thought itself.

This thinking can only destroy metaphysical ideas, it cannot produce them. It finds no home, either in the world or in a cogitated realm of transcendence. Metaphysical speculation is extinct, mythical thinking has become meaningless. But as long as the world endures, metaphysics and myth remain; they are the fuel which must forever be consumed anew.

Stcherbatsky contrasts the Buddhist antimetaphysical philosophy with the metaphysical philosophy of the Vedanta. Both deny the reality of the world. But though the Buddhist denies the reality of the world of appearance, he remains within it, because beyond it begins a realm that is inaccessible to our insight. The Vedantist on the other hand denies the reality of the world of appearance only in order to establish the true being of Brahman. The Buddhist says: Knowledge is undivided; only to our deluded eye does it present itself in the cleavage of subject and object. The Vedantist says, however: The whole world is a simple substance that never ceases; the division of consciousness into subject and object is mere illusion.

5. *The state of Perfect Wisdom:* It is called freedom from conflict. The thinking which, forever in conflict, negates every statement, is directed toward the place where all conflict ceases, where "dwells" the unconflicting (*Pr.* 36, 54). The seeker after wisdom is bidden to "dwell in the unconflicting." What kind of state is this?

It is described: when the work is done and the task carried out, the burden is cast off; that is the goal. Thoughts are made free, mastery over all thought is gained in the detached knowledge which masters itself. The fetters of existence have vanished, impurities fall away, freedom from torment is achieved (*Pr.* 34).

Through passion and the deception of signs, all the *dharmas* bring about suffering. Once the emptiness of suffering is perceived, it is overcome. Now man has achieved a state free both from illusion and from torment. In this perfect peace the emptiness of the *dharmas* does not cease to exist, but I am no longer touched by them, they have lost their terrors, their poison, their power. In emptiness I gain awareness of that to which signs such as birth and death no longer apply, of something motionless, for which all coming and going have lost their meaning.

This attitude is not what is ordinarily known as skepticism. For the operations of thought which lead beyond the antinomy of true and false, that is, beyond thought, also carry it beyond dogmatism and skepticism. To call it negativism is to fail to see that here the no as well as the yes has vanished. To call it nihilism is to forget that the alternative between being and nothingness has been dismissed.

How in Perfect Wisdom "being" is experienced as the emptiness of the world is illustrated in images. To the Bodhisattva all things are like an echo, he does not think them, he does not see them, he does not know them (*Pr.* 75). He lives in the world as in the "emptiness of a city of ghosts" (*Nag.* 27). The "illusory nature" of things, the fact that they at once are and are not (and are adequately conceived in none of the four views), is compared with the materializations (regarded as real in India) of a magician (*Pr.* 46): a magician at a crossroads conjures up a large crowd of people and makes them disappear again; so is the world. No one has been killed or destroyed by the magician; so without destroying them, the Bodhisattva makes multitudes of beings disappear.

The Bodhisattva knows, sees, and believes all things by virtue of a concept which is contained neither in the concept of a thing (*dharma*) nor of a non-thing (*adharma*). The right attitude would be achieved by one who could fully explain lines like the following: "The stars, darkness, a light, an illusion, dew, a bubble, a dream, a streak of lightning, a cloud" (*Pr.* 157).

In keeping with this attitude worldly values are disparaged. The Buddha is quoted as saying: "In my eyes the dignity of a king or prince is no more than a grain of dust in the sun; in my eyes a treasure of gold and jewels is no more than clay and shards . . . in my eyes the thousand systems of the cosmos are no more than the fruit of the myrobalan . . . in my eyes the ritual objects (of Buddhism) are no more than a heap of worthless treasures . . . in my eyes the path of the Buddhas is no more than the sight of a flower . . . in my eyes Nirvana is no more than a waking from sleep by day or night . . . in my eyes the error and truth (of the various schools) is no more than the game of the six dragons" (Hackmann).

Are we entitled to say that the possessor of such wisdom sees nothing but a vast unutterable nothingness? That he is submerged in the shoreless ocean of the undifferentiated? We must hesitate. The thinker whose aim is redemption from the fetters of the *dharmas* is beyond our understanding and our judgment. "His way, like that of the birds in the air, is hard to follow" (*Dhammapada* 92). But it is certain that in perversions of the original thought futility and meaninglessness soon make their appearance.

6. *The perversions:* The attitude of superiority to world and self in the emptiness of Perfect Wisdom becomes ambiguous:

Sovereign "emptiness" is open to every fulfillment, hence never fulfilled in life and never at an end. One who takes this attitude looks upon life from a distance, countenances fulfillment but never succumbs to it, accepts it but is never moved. Present, he is always beyond; in satisfaction he experiences boundless dissatisfaction, which receives only the reflected radiance of the realm against which all finite strivings shatter. Thus in the temporal world such an attitude, although sustained by quietness in the source, is open, that is, mobile, active, concerned, but all actions are considered by a standard which destroys their reality. But this emptiness can be perverted. This occurs when all existence vanishes in the quiet of nothingness. Then my own existence shrivels in time, because all fulfillment is rejected in favor of an abstract fulfillment of being–notbeing, of emptiness, of quiet as such. When the fuel of veiled truth is no longer present, the combustion process leading to the unfathomable depths of Nirvana can no longer take place. Along with the fuel, with the reality of existence, the language of understanding vanishes; the consequence is a fall into the incommunicable.

This possibility of perversion is seen in Western terms. The philosophical texts of Nagarjuna describe the perversion of Perfect Wisdom in a manner consonant with his own thinking. Since everything that is said from the standpoint of Perfect Wisdom is open to misunderstanding, it is immediately misused. Consequently, the liberation of men in the course of generations is not an advance; rather, misunderstanding leads to ruin.

On the whole the prognosis is unfavorable. "After Buddha's Nirvana, after five hundred years in a *dharma* that is mere imitation, after the minds of men have gradually grown dull, they no longer recognize Buddha's meaning and cling only to words and written characters" (*Nag.* II, 2). How does this come about? They hear and speak of absolute emptiness but do not understand its source. They express such skeptical thoughts as: If all is empty, how can we distinguish the consequences of good and evil? They can ask such questions only from a worldly point of view, because for the worldly there is no difference between worldly truth and absolute truth. In other words, what was intended speculatively they understand as purposive knowledge. In objectivizing thought, they lose the meaning of the doctrine of emptiness, because, in their attachment to mere logical propositions, they draw conclusions that have nothing to do with emptiness. They fail to understand that to include the Buddha, the doctrine, the congregation in emptiness, is not to deny them but to consider them as *dharma* and as such to bring them into a state of suspension. Such a state of suspension is possible only if we refrain from absolutizing any representation, idea, or proposition. This is to travel the true path, in *dharma,* toward the disappearance of suffering in Perfect Wisdom. Thus to look upon all things as without absolute being is the profoundest elucidation of world and self. But they lose this light by their attachment to the word of the doctrine. Ceasing to take the doctrine as a sign, an indicator, and looking upon it as an object of knowledge, they lose the thought.

Concern with the profound doctrine is salutary, but also dangerous. When it is not properly understood, it kills. For if emptiness is seen imperfectly, it leads those of little understanding not only into error but into destruction, just as poisonous snakes, if improperly handled, and magic and conjuring if improperly executed, lead to destruction (*Nag.* I, 151).

What emptiness ultimately came to mean in popular Buddhism is shown by a Chinese book of wisdom written in the twelfth century: He who has understood the emptiness of corporeal things ceases to set any store by opinions; he will refrain from all activity and sit still without a thought (Hackmann).

7. *The original consciousness of the Encompassing:* This strange thinking does not have an object, knowledge of which is gained through reasons and facts. Its presupposition is not a thesis but the Encompassing, which is manifested through figures of thought and metaphors. All ideas are immersed in an atmosphere without which they would wither away. They throw light on the presupposed attitude of the thinker, which without this thinking he would be unable to maintain.

The fundamental view is seemingly gained by logical thought. The intention is to destroy logic with logic and so demonstrate that thinking is itself illusion; to prove that nothing can be proved, that nothing can be asserted, and that nothingness can also not be asserted.

With all this, logical necessities are discovered, which have validity as such. But they are no more than a rational game, concerning which it must be asked: Why play it?

In the Asian form of this thinking, we see a surface picture which misleads us as to the origin: in discussion, whatever another may assert is denied. There is a triumphant consciousness of destruction, against which nothing can stand up. By the same endlessly repeated tricks, everything that is said is shown to be untenable. Behind these playful abuses lies the true meaning, namely, that all statements concerning being and nonbeing must be transcended in the unconflicting. The self-destruction of all thought must free us for something else. This something else can be fulfilled by experience in the higher meditative techniques of Yoga. But it is also accessible to normal consciousness. Where emptiness is actualized, things are suspended between being and nonbeing; then they point to something which is inexpressible but experienced with full certainty.

This Encompassing cannot be described as an empirical psychological state, but it can be adumbrated. Schayer attempts to give an idea of it by indicating the senses in which certain words were originally employed. *"Shunyata"* (emptiness) is employed as a stage of meditation (in the Pali Canon): "And now let him catch sight of an empty village, and let every house he enters be forsaken, deserted, and empty; and let every dish he touches be empty and without content." Here man's sensibility is likened to an empty village; this emptiness does not signify a denial of being, but indifference, insipidity, imperviousness. *"Animitta"* ("without definite suchness," "signlessness") means in the Pali Canon: nonattachment to the attributes of perceived things; it does not mean a denial of their existence, but a mode of practical behavior, in which the monk, like a vigilant gatekeeper, bars access to the sensory stimuli streaming in on him from without. "Maya" (magic) means comparison of the world to a phantasm, as an expression of the arbitrariness and futility of being, not as a denial of its reality. Here it should not be forgotten that the Indians looked upon images, echoes, and dreams as realities. Existence is not denied; what is denied is its authenticity.

8. Survey of the Buddhist sects and the ultimate meaning of all doctrines: The Shunyavadins are one sect among many. What is common to all is the Buddhist striving for redemption, the knowledge of suffering and of the insignificance of the world's reality. On this common ground, reflection on the possibility of knowing reality had resulted in numerous opinions:

The outside world is real and can be known directly through perception (the Sarvastivadins); it is not perceived by the senses but its existence can be inferred through perceptions (the Sautrantikas); only consciousness is certain and the source of this certainty is consciousness itself; only the inner world is real, the difference between subject and object has no real existence (the Yogacaras); neither outside nor inner world can be recognized as real, independent being; there is no difference between subjective and objective reality (the Shunyavadins, to which Nagarjuna belonged).

In this schema of "epistemological" standpoints we can recognize the Western schema of idealism and realism, rationalism and empiricism, positivism and nihilism, especially in reference to the question of the reality of the outside world. But such comparisons apply only to the rational by-products of the philosophical operations effected by the Indian thinkers. Obviously, the essential cannot be appropriately expressed in terms of a formulable doctrine. This would be possible if the instrument of salvation were a definite knowledge. But since all knowledge in the sense of positively formulable contents signifies "attachment," the way of salvation is to be sought rather in the shattering of all knowledge, all possibility of knowledge, and all opinions.

The emptiness of all worldly reality becomes the positive being of the source, whence man fell into the coming-and-going, the evil and suffering of the world, and to which he must return. All thinking and all being-thought pertain to the fall. The aim of true thinking is a return from the unfolding of thought to nonthinking. What happened through the unfolding of thought can be undone by better thought in the dissolution of thought. The final step is to perceive the untruth of all signs and hence of language. Once it is understood that a word is a mere sign without real meaning, the word disappears, and that is deliverance. Consciousness, which created suffering by shaping emptiness into the many worlds, is carried back to its source.

But in the world there still remain doctrine, language, the teaching of the way of salvation, the disintegration of thought by the same thought that brought about the fall by thought. Consequently, despite all the insight a philosopher could gain into his own thinking by the self-annulment of thinking, he could not help taking a position—unless the need for silence were taken seriously and all discourse, all listening, all communication ceased. And so Nagarjuna's position, his doctrine of "conditioned becoming," became a fixed formula for emptiness.

The sense of this doctrine of "conditioned becoming" is that since everything at once is and is not, everything is conditional. Because he knows this, the Bodhisattva becomes master of all thoughts, enslaved to none. Moving among finite thoughts, he hovers over them, and in this state of suspension he includes himself and his own existence. I myself and my thinking are the condition of all things and of the phantasm which is the existence of this world. This world of the *dharmas* and the self as well are conditioned. The process of conditioned becoming produces a world in which we think ourselves at home and at the same time suffer without hope of surcease. But we see through this whole world of conditioned becoming, including the formulated doctrine, and that is salvation. The illusion recedes and that of which it is impossible to speak lies open before us. The doctrine is the ferryboat that will carry us across the river of existence. Once we have reached the other shore, the boat is superfluous. Since the doctrine belongs to the illusory stream of worldly existence, to take it along with us on the other side would be as foolish as to carry the boat on our shoulders as we leave the shore to enter the new country. The Sage abandons it to the stream which lies behind him. The doctrine is useful in helping us to escape, but there is nothing to be gained by holding it fast.

Historical Comparisons

When we compare different forms of thought, analogies merely accentuate the differences in historical content.

A. *Dialectic:* Dialectic is the movement of thought through opposition and contradiction, but this can mean very different things: it may lead by way of contradictions to limits, at which it discloses the abyss but also an open horizon; the situation at the limit becomes a goal and a demand.—It may lead to closed circles, in which contradictions are transcended in a synthesis; all the stages of the thought process are integrated into a living totality.—It may be conceived and carried out as a reality, in which negation as such yields a positive result by the negation of the negation; the new is expected to be born automatically from negative thought and action.

None of these possibilities is essential in the dialectic of the Buddhists. Here dialectic becomes a means of rising above thought to the unthinkable, which, measured by thinking, is neither being nor nothingness, but both in equal degree, though even in such statements it remains beyond our grasp.

Sometimes Nietzsche seems to approach this method. He, too, prevents us from coming to rest in any position. He flings us into a whirl of oppositions, and at some time negates every statement he makes by its opposite. In this way he has created in the modern world a spiritual situation which he himself brought about in the belief that the best way to overcome nihilism was to carry it to its ultimate consequences. But Nietzsche, who without systematically elaborating this dialectic set out to employ it as an instrument for the complete liberation of mankind, conceived of this liberation as a step not into an unthinkable otherness, but rather into a worldly reality, the full and unconditional possession of which he thought he was making possible. When Nietzsche said: Nothing is true, everything is permissible, he aspired to open men's minds, not to a transcendence which he denied, but to the earth and the ascent of man in his own earthly world, through himself and beyond himself—beyond good and evil.

Like the Buddhists, Nietzsche tried to break down all the categories. There is, he said, no unity, no causality, no substance, no subject, etc. All these are useful fictions, perhaps indispensable to life. Of all things, says Nagarjuna, none exists in itself, no thought or object of thought is true, all are conditioned. Both agree that there is no being; everything is mere interpretation. But in this form of thought that is common to them, in their negative operations, they pursue very different aims. To determine the true nature of these aims is for us a never-ending task. In Nagarjuna and the Buddhists the stated aim is Nirvana and the will to salvation; in Nietzsche it is the will to power and the will to engender a superman.

B. *The structure of being, the categories:* The Buddhists have their so-called formula of causality (the circle of the fundamental categories of being). The Yogacaras speak in particular of the primordial consciousness, the germinal consciousness, whose unfolding brings with it the illusion of the world. The development of this idea shows the nature and form of a world that does not truly exist, the structure of all appearances. This Indian conception has been likened to Western idealism. And indeed, Kant conceives the whole world as appearance, its forms defined by the categories of consciousness as such. All knowable objects are produced, not as to their being but as to their forms, by the subject. So-called transcendental idealism created a systematic schema of this reality that unfolds in thought.

But the analogy at once discloses a difference. The Indians devised this structure in order to divest scientific knowledge of its truth, for it is dream and illusion. Kant conceived and developed his similar structure in order to justify scientific knowledge within the limits of possible experience. For him the world is appearance, but not illusion. The idealists who followed Kant did not conceive these categorial structures as limited to appearance, but as the eternal truth itself, as God's thoughts. Neither view bears any kinship to Buddhist thinking. For the German idealists justify knowledge of the world and activity in the world, while the Buddhists on the contrary stand for abandonment of the world, for renunciation of scientific knowledge, which they look upon as unrewarding because fundamentally false; they reject action in shaping the world, which is not only futile but holds us in a state of captivity.

C. *Emptiness and openness:* Emptiness permits of the greatest openness, the greatest willingness to accept the things of the world as a starting point from which to make the great leap. Indifference toward all worldly things also leaves every possibility open. Hence the tolerance of Buddhism toward other religions, modes of life, views of the world. The Buddhist lives with all these as expressions of a lower, worldly truth, each equally satisfactory as a point of departure toward higher things. This unrestricted openness attracts men. Buddhism won Asia; though repressed here and there, it never resorted to violence, never forced dogmas on anyone. Buddhism had no religious wars, no inquisition, and never engaged in the secular politics of an organized church.

Western reason presents an analogy to this Buddhist mode of thought, which is as infinitely open as emptiness. Both listen, both respect the opinions of others. But the difference is this: the Buddhist Sage goes through the world like a duck; he no longer gets wet. He has transcended the world by dropping it. He seeks fulfillment in an unthinkable unworld. For Western man, however, reason finds its fulfillment, not in any absolute, but in the historicity of the world itself, which he gathers into his own Existenz. Only in historical realization, becoming identical with it, does he find his ground; he knows that this is the source of his freedom and of his relation to transcendence.

D. *Detachment:* Detachment from the world and myself, the inner liberation that I achieve by dissociating myself from everything that happens to me in the world and everything I myself do, think, and am, is a form which was embodied in very different ways.

The Bhagavad Gita praises the warrior who remains indifferent and aloof despite his impetuous heroism, who plays the game conscientiously and acts energetically, while regarding all activity as vain.—In Epicurus the fundamental attitude is: I have passions, but they do not have me.—In St. Paul, I act and live in the world as though I were not there.—Nietzsche regards detachment from oneself as the hallmark of the aristocratic soul.

Despite this analogy in the form of detachment, the fundamental attitude of the Buddhists and of Nagarjuna is an entirely different one: the accent is on the impersonal; as the world becomes a matter of indifference, the self is extinguished. The detachment has its source not in a "myself," but in a transcendent reality which is not a self.

In all Western forms of detachment from the world, the essential is sought in something that is present in the world: in the empty freedom of a punctual self, or in a self which in historical immersion, in self-identification, takes upon itself the burden of being-given-to-oneself but nevertheless illumines itself infinitely and achieves self-detachment in reflection.

Considered from the standpoint of Asian thought, these forms of detachment will always be imperfect, for they all preserve a bond with the world. From the Western standpoint, however, the Asian form will always seem to be an escape from the world into the inaccessible and incommunicable.

BIBLIOGRAPHY

EDITOR'S NOTE:
The Bibliography is based on that given in the German original. English translations are given wherever possible. Selected English and American works have been added; these are marked by an asterisk.

The Pre-Socratics:
Anaximander—Heraclitus—Parmenides

SOURCES:

Diels, Hermann: *Die Fragmente der Vorsokratiker, griechisch und deutsch,* ed. with additions by W. Kranz. 3 vols. 6th ed. Berlin, Weidmannsche Verlagsbuchhandlung, 1956–9.

*Freeman, Kathleen: *Ancilla to the Pre-Socratic Philosophers: A Complete Translation of the Fragments in Diels, Fragmente der Vorsokratiker.* Oxford, Blackwell, 1956.

*Kirk, G. S., and J. E. Raven: *The Presocratic Philosophers: A Critical History with a Selection of Texts* (in Greek and English). Cambridge, Cambridge University Press, 1962.

Diogenes Laertius: *Lives of Eminent Philosophers,* trans. by Robert Drew Hicks. (Loeb Classical Library.) 2 vols. Cambridge, Mass., Harvard University Press; London, Wm. Heinemann, Ltd., 1950.

Capelle, Wilhelm: *Die Vorsokratiker: Die Fragmente und Quellenberichte.* Leipzig, Kröner, 1935.

Nestle, Wilhelm: *Die griechischen Philosophen.* Vol. 1: *Die Vorsokratiker.* Jena, E. Diederichs, 1908; 4th ed., Düsseldorf-Cologne, E. Diederichs, 1956. Vol. 2: *Die Sokratiker.* Jena, E. Diederichs, 1923. Vols. 3–4: *Die Nachsokratiker.* Jena, E. Diederichs, 1923.

Grünwald, Michael: *Die Anfänge der abendländischen Philosophie: Fragmente und Lehrberichte der Vorsokratiker.* Zurich, Artemis-Verlag, 1949.

Snell, Bruno: *Heraklit: Fragmente, Griechisch und Deutsch.* Munich, Heimeran Verlag, 1926; 2d ed., Munich, Heimeran Verlag, 1940.

Parmenides, in *Plato and Parmenides,* trans. with introduction and running commentary by Francis Macdonald Cornford. London, Routledge & Kegan Paul; New York, Liberal Arts Press, 1957.

SECONDARY WORKS:

Bernays, Jacob: *Die heraklitischen Briefe: Ein Beitrag zur philosophischen und religionsgeschichtlichen Literatur.* Berlin and London, 1869.

Burnet, John: *Early Greek Philosophy.* London, A. & C. Black, 1892; 4th ed. London, A. & C. Black, 1930; New York, Meridian Books, 1957.

*Cherniss, Harold Frederick: *Aristotle's Criticism of Presocratic Philosophy.* Baltimore, Johns Hopkins Press, 1935.

*Cornford, Francis Macdonald: *Principium Sapientiae: The Origin of Greek Philosophical Thought,* ed. by W. K. C. Guthrie. Cambridge, Cambridge University Press, 1952.

———: *Plato and Parmenides.* London, Routledge & Kegan Paul; New York, Liberal Arts Press, 1957.

Fränkel, Hermann Ferdinand: *Wege und Formen frühgriechischen Denkens.* Munich, Beck, 1955; 2d ed., Munich, Beck, 1962.

*———: *Dichtung und Philosophie des frühen Griechentums: Eine Geschichte der griechischen Literatur von Homer bis Pindar.* (American Philological Association, Philological Monographs, No. 13.) New York, American Philological Association, 1951.

*Freeman, Kathleen: *The Pre-Socratic Philosophers: A Companion to Diels, Fragmente der Vorsokratiker.* 3d ed. Oxford, Blackwell, 1953.

Fritz, Kurt von: "*Nous, noein* and Their Derivatives in Pre-Socratic Philosophy (excluding Anaxagoras)," in *Classical Philology,* XL (October, 1945), 223–42; XLI (January, 1946), 12–34.

Gigon, Olof Alfred: *Untersuchungen zu Heraklit.* Leipzig, Diederich'sche Verlagsbuchhandlung, 1935.

———: *Der Ursprung der griechischen Philosophie von Hesiod bis Parmenides.* Basel, Benno Schwabe, 1945.

Jaeger, Werner: *Paideia: The Ideals of Greek Culture,* trans. by Gilbert Highet. 3 vols. New York, Oxford University Press, 1944.

———: *The Theology of the Early Greek Philosophers,* trans. by Edward S. Robinson. New York, Oxford University Press, 1947.

*Kirk, G. S.: "Some Problems in Anaximander," in *Classical Quarterly,* New Series V (1955), 21–38.

*———: *Heraclitus: The Cosmic Fragments.* Cambridge, Cambridge University Press, 1954.

Nebel, Gerhard: "Das Sein des Parmenides," in *Der Bund, Jahrbuch,* pp. 87–119. Wuppertal, Marées Verlag, 1947.

Reich, Klaus, "Anaximander und Parmenides," in *Marburger Winckelmann-Programm, 1950–51,* pp. 13 ff.

Reinhardt, Karl: *Parmenides und die Geschichte der griechischen Philosophie.* 2d ed. Frankfurt am Main, V. Klostermann, 1959.

Riezler, Kurt: *Parmenides.* Frankfurt am Main, V. Klostermann, 1934.

*Snell, Bruno: *The Discovery of the Mind: The Greek Origins of European Thought,* trans. by T. G. Rosenmeyer. Oxford, Blackwell, 1953.

*Vlastos, Gregory: "On Heraclitus," in *American Journal of Philology,* LXXVI (1955), 337–68.

Zeller, Eduard: *Die Philosophie der Griechen.* 3 vols. in 6. Leipzig, O. R. Reisland, 1920–3.

Plotinus

SOURCES:

Plotini Opera, ed. Paul Henry and Hans-Rudolf Schwyzer. *Porphyrii vita Plotini; Ennéades I–V.* 2 vols. Paris, Desclée de Brouwer, 1951–9.

Ennéades. Vols. I–VI, text and French trans. by Émile Bréhier. Paris, Société d'édition "Les belles lettres," 1956–63.

Schriften, trans. into German by Richard Harder. 5 vols. Leipzig, Meiner, 1930–7.

Schriften, text and German trans. with commentary. 5 vols. Hamburg, F. Meiner, 1956–64.

*The Enneads, trans. by Stephen MacKenna. 3d ed., rev. by R. S. Page, with foreword by E. R. Dodds and introduction by Paul Henry. London, Faber and Faber, 1962; New York, Pantheon Books, Inc., n.d.

Longinus: *On the Sublime,* trans. by A. O. Prickard. Oxford, Clarendon Press, 1906.

SECONDARY WORKS:

Alföldi, Andreas: "Die Vorherrschaft der Pannonier im Römerreich und die Reaktion des Hellenentums unter Gallienus," in *Fünfundzwanzig Jahre Römisch-Germanische Kommission.* Berlin, 1930.

***Armstrong, Arthur Hilary: *The Architecture of the Intelligible Universe in the Philosophy of Plotinus.* Cambridge, Cambridge University Press, 1940.

Bréhier, Émile: *La Philosophie de Plotin.* Paris, Boivin, 1928. English trans.: *The Philosophy of Plotinus,* trans. by Joseph Thomas. Chicago, University of Chicago Press, 1958.

Dodds, E. R.: "The *Parmenides* of Plato and the Origin of the Neoplatonic 'One,' " in *Classical Quarterly* (London), XXII (1928), 129–42.

***Henry, Paul: *Plotin et l'Occident.* Louvain, "Spicilegium sacrum lovaniense," 1934.

***Inge, William Ralph: *The Philosophy of Plotinus.* 2 vols. 3d ed. London and New York, Longmans, Green, 1929.

Kirchner, Carl Hermann: *Die Philosophie des Plotin. Halle,* H. W. Schmid, 1854.

Kristeller, Paul Oskar: *Der Begriff der Seele in der Ethik des Plotin.* Tübingen, Mohr, 1929.

Nebel, Gerhard: *Plotins Kategorien der intelligiblen Welt: Ein Beitrag zur Geschichte der Idee.* Tübingen, Mohr, 1929.

Oppermann, Hans: *Plotins Leben: Untersuchungen zur Biographie Plotins.* Heidelberg, C. Winter, 1929.

Richter, Arthur: *Neu-Platonische Studien.* 5 vols. Halle, Schmidt, 1864–7.

Rodenwaldt, Gerhart: "Zur Kunstgeschichte der Jahre 220 bis 270," in *Jahrbuch des Deutschen Archäologischen Instituts,* Vol. LI, 1936.

***Schwyzer, Hans Rudolf: "Plotinos," in *Realencyclopädie der classischen Altertumswissenschaft,* ed. by Pauly-Wissowa, Kroll, Ziegler, Vol. XXI. Stuttgart, J. B. Metzler, 1951.

Lao-tzu

SOURCES:

Tao te King, German trans. with commentary and introduction by Victor von Strauss. Leipzig, Fr. Fleischer, 1870; reprinted, Leipzig, Verlag der "Asia Major," 1924.

Lao-tszes Buch vom höchsten Wesen und vom höchsten Gut (*Tao-te-king*), trans. with introduction and commentary by Julius Grill. Tübingen, Mohr, 1910.

Laotse, Tao te King, das Buch des Alten vom Sinn und Leben, trans. with commentary and introduction by Richard Wilhelm. Jena, E. Diederichs, 1913.

*Lin Yutang, trans.: *The Wisdom of Laotse.* New York, Random House, Modern Library, 1948.

Chan, Wing-tsit, trans.: *The Way of Lao Tzu.* Indianapolis, Bobbs-Merrill Company, Inc., 1963.

Nagarjuna

SOURCES:

Die Buddhistische Philosophie in ihrer geschichtlichen Entwicklung. 4 vols. Heidelberg, C. Winter, 1904–27. Vol. 2: *Die mittlere Lehre des Nagarjuna,* trans. from the Tibetan version by Max Walleser (1911). Vol. 3: *Die mittlere Lehre des Nagarjuna,* trans. from the Chinese version by Max Walleser (1912).

*Radhakrishnan, Sarvepalli: *Indian Philosophy,* Vol. I. New York, Humanities Press, 1958.

INDEX OF NAMES

Ameinias, 19
Amelius, 32
Ammonios Saccas, 32, 33, 83
Anaxagoras, 25
Anaximander, 3–8, 9, 18, 22, 28, 30, 31
Aphrodite, 69
Archilochos, 15
Aristotle, 5, 18, 35, 37, 44, 51, 83, 84
Asanga, 115
Augustine, St., 85

Bernays, Jacob, 30
Bodhidharma, 121
Bréhier, Émile, 34
Buddha, 111, 115–120, 124, 126–127
Burnet, John, 4

Calderón, 6, 70
Ch'in Shih Huang-Ti, 112–113
Chuang-tzu, 87, 98, 111–112
Chu Hsi, 111
Cicero, 7
Circe, 69
Confucius, 87, 98, 100, 101, 111
Constantine I, Emperor, 32
Cusanus, see Nicholas of Cusa

Damascius, 85
Democritus, 25
Dharmakirti, 115
Dignaga, 115
Dikē, 13, 19, 21, 24
Diocletian, Emperor, 32
Dionysus, 12, 69
Dodds, E. R., 85

Empedocles, 23, 25
Epicurus, 132
Erinyes, 13
Eros, 22
Eupalinos, 3
Euripides, 17

Ficino, Marsilius, 86
Forke, Alfred, 87

Gallienus, Emperor, 32–33, 85
Goethe, Johann, 23
Gordianus, Emperor, 32
Groot, J. J. M. de, 88

Hackmann, 121, 126, 127
Harder, Richard, 85
Hecataeus, 15
Hegel, Georg, 18, 54
Heraclitus, 7, 8, 9–18, 22, 23, 28–31, 83, 84,
    101
Herakles, 69
Hermodoros, 15
Hesiod, 15, 28
Homer, 15, 27

Iamblichus, 85

Jäger, Albert, 12
Jeremiah, 101
Jesus Christ, 18
John, St., 18

Kant, Immanuel, 26, 40, 53, 88, 131

Lao-tzu, 87–114
Lassalle, Ferdinand, 18
Liang Wu Ti, Emperor, 121–122
Lieh-tzu, 88
Luther, Martin, 40

Marx, Karl, 18
Mencius, 87
Mo Ti, 87

Nagarjuna, 115–132
Narcissus, 69
Nicholas of Cusa, 56
Nietzsche, Friedrich, 6, 18, 27, 29, 31,
    130–131, 132

Odysseus, 69
Oldenberg, Hermann, 116
Olympius, 33

Pandora, 69
Parmenides, 8, 9, 18, 19–31, 83, 84
Paul, St., 132
Phalaris, 79
Philip "the Arabian," Emperor, 32
Philo, 18, 85
Plato, 7, 26–27, 35, 41, 51, 55, 63, 70, 78, 81, 83–86, 88, 123
Plotinus, 23, 32–86
Porphyry, 33, 49, 85
Poseidonius, 84
Proclus, 85
Pseudo-Dionysius Areopagita, 85
Pythagoras, 15

Reich, Klaus, 30
Rohde, Erwin, 6

Salonina, Empress, 32
Schayer, 128
Schelling, Friedrich, 27, 54
Shih Huang-Ti, 106

Simplicius, 5, 85
Socrates, 17, 77
Solon, 6
Spinoza, Baruch, 6, 44, 88
Ssŭ-ma Ch'ien, 87, 101
Stcherbatsky, T., 124
Strauss, Victor von, 88, 100, 109

Tertullian, 85
Thales, 5
Themis, 21

Uranus, 69

Vasubandhu, 115

Wittgenstein, Ludwig, 123

Xenophanes, 7, 15, 28, 84

Zethos, 33
Zeus, 13, 69